Training teachers to work in schools considered difficult

Jean-Louis AUDUC

Paris 1998
UNESCO: International Institute for Educational Planning

The Swedish International Development Co-operation Agency (Sida) has provided financial assistance for the publication of this booklet.

Published in 1998 by the United Nations
Educational, Scientific and Cultural Organization
7 place de Fontenoy, 75700 Paris
Printed in France by Stedi, 75018 Paris

Cover design by Bruno Pfäffli
ISBN 92-803-1169-7

Fundamentals of educational planning – 59

WITHDRAWN

* Also published in French. Other titles to appear.

Fundamentals of educational planning

The booklets in this series are written primarily for two types of clientele: those engaged in educational planning and administration, in developing as well as developed countries; and others, less specialized, such as senior government officials and policy-makers who seek a more general understanding of educational planning and of how it is related to overall national development. They are intended to be of use either for private study or in formal training programmes.

Since this series was launched in 1967 practices and concepts of educational planning have undergone substantial change. Many of the assumptions which underlay earlier attempts to rationalise the process of educational development have been criticised or abandoned. Even if rigid mandatory centralized planning has now clearly proven to be inappropriate, this does not mean that all forms of planning have been dispensed with. On the contrary, the need for collecting data, evaluating the efficiency of existing programmes, undertaking a wide range of studies, exploring the future and fostering broad debate on these bases to guide educational policy and decision-making has become even more acute than before.

The scope of educational planning has been broadened. In addition to the formal system of education, it is now applied to all other important educational efforts in non-formal settings. Attention to the growth and expansion of education systems is being comple-mented and sometimes even replaced by a growing concern for the quality of the entire educational process and for the control of its results. Finally, planners and administrators have become more and more aware of the importance of implementation strategies and of the role of different regulatory mechanisms in this respect: the choice of financing methods, the examination and certification procedures or various other regulation and incentive structures. The concern of planners is twofold: to reach a better understanding of the validity of education in its own empirically observed specific dimensions and to help in defining appropriate strategies for change.

The purpose of these booklets includes monitoring the evolution and change in educational policies and their effect upon educational planning requirements; highlighting current issues of educational planning and analysing them in the context of their historical and societal setting; and disseminating methodologies of planning which can be applied in the context of both the developed and the developing countries.

In order to help the Institute identify the real up-to-date issues in educational planning and policy-making in different parts of the world, an Editorial Board has been appointed, composed of two general editors and associate editors from different regions, all professionals of high repute in their own field. At the first meeting of this new Editorial Board in January 1990, its members identified key topics to be covered in the coming issues under the following headings:

1. Education and development.
2. Equity considerations.
3. Quality of education.
4. Structure, administration and management of education.
5. Curriculum.
6. Cost and financing of education.
7. Planning techniques and approaches.
8. Information systems, monitoring and evaluation.

Each heading is covered by one or two associate editors.

The series has been carefully planned but no attempt has been made to avoid differences or even contradictions in the views expressed by the authors. The Institute itself does not wish to impose any official doctrine. Thus, while the views are the responsibility of the authors and may not always be shared by UNESCO or the IIEP, they warrant attention in the international forum of ideas. Indeed, one of the purposes of this series is to reflect a diversity of experience and opinions by giving different authors from a wide range of backgrounds and disciplines the opportunity of expressing their views on changing theories and practices in educational planning.

In every country a great number of children live under very difficult conditions, and are subject to (even in the family environment) violent treatment. Violence is ubiquitous. It is particularly visible in the ghettos, on the outskirts or in the inner cities. But it also exists in rural areas. It is now appearing in schools and many teachers are faced with classes termed 'difficult'. The school, whose job it is to impart the knowledge which should enable youth to evade poverty, which should teach values such as peace and tolerance, is itself not sheltered from society's troubles.

Violence at school has become a real problem in a number of developed countries where school attendance is obligatory up to the age of 16 or 18 years old. One can no longer exclude pupils as was done in the past, and as is still the case in certain countries where the economic conditions (notably high unemployment levels and the development of marginality) do not allow the channelling of energies towards employment. It is certainly true that violence in the school reflects what is going on outside the school. But it also shows that the contents of teaching and its methods, very often developed for the chosen and privileged few, are inadequate for mass education with the wide variety in the level of knowledge and expectations and and for those with specific interests and cultures.

This booklet written by Jean-Louis Auduc addresses the need to better prepare young teachers to work in classes or schools considered difficult. They need to be trained to face up to unpredictable situations and they need to learn how to listen to their pupils. Moreover, they have to take it upon themselves to create winning scenarios for the pupils, rather than discourage them. Finally, they need to know how to work with other actors in the school.

As the author highlights, there are no miracle solutions or tested methods which can be applied in all contexts, in all situations and to all cultures. Many pedagogical innovations are being tried out but have not yet been evaluated. Rather than list these methods, this booklet addresses itself to decision-makers and managers of education in different countries to alert them of the dire need to consider this phenomena and to adapt teacher training programmes. It might also lead one to reflect on the 'violence' directed at young people by certain humiliating and rigid school practices which should be reconsidered.

In certain cases, the recommendations go beyond preparing teachers for difficult audiences and deal with training of all teachers who have to modify their teaching practices to take into consideration the specific characteristics of their pupils. This booklet will be of as much interest to teachers as planners and managers in education.

The Institute would like to thank Jean-Louis Auduc, Deputy Director of the *Institut universitaire de formation des maîtres de Créteil* for having accepted to write this booklet. We are equally grateful to Jean-Claude Eicher, Professor at the University of Burgundy, the associate editor responsible for this publication, for his highly active participation in its preparation.

Jacques Hallak
Assistant Director-General, UNESCO
Director, IIEP

9

Preface

School is no longer what it was!

After a difficult period of gestation, the idea that all children should receive basic education, as far as possible in the same conditions, became the norm in all developed countries between the middle of the nineteenth and the start of the twentieth century.

Yet this obligation related only to young children and, as a rule, was associated with authoritarian prescriptive practice that attached central importance to the institution and school teachers responsible for imparting basic knowledge to all, together with common values defined by the nation. Pupils had to fall in with this strict framework. Their task was to learn and to obey.

However, circumstances changed, as the period of compulsory schooling became longer while, more generally, a growing and ultimately dominant proportion of young people completed secondary schooling.

In the first instance, pupils with a broader range of intellectual abilities continued secondary schooling. Thus, authoritarian uniform teaching methods were increasingly less effective in the classroom. Teachers were obliged to resort on a trial and error basis, and with varying degrees of success, to a 'differentiated approach' that took account of individual pupil characteristics.

However, near universal schooling for the adolescent age group also brought into the classroom young people from very different backgrounds, especially particular groups whose parents had never been educated beyond primary school, and whose culture was markedly different from the one to which they were now exposed. The tensions related to this discontinuity of experience were aggravated by two other phenomena: immigration from countries whose culture was further removed from that of the host country than in the preceding period, and the contemporary economic crisis. Secondary schools have found it particularly difficult to contend with the deep-seated inability of a significant group of pupils to relate to school curricula and, increasingly, with their often violent reaction for school seen as the agency of a society which rejected them.

It is vital, therefore, for future teachers to be prepared for their profession in a different way. The re-enactment of what these newcomers to teaching experienced when they themselves were at school will now only yield satisfactory results in a minority of 'privileged classes'. Admittedly, it is only in a minority of classes ambiguously termed 'difficult', that problems are really acute to the extent that some consider the situation to be virtually hopeless. Yet diversity is virtually omnipresent, while the rift between the culture of most young people and that of their teachers has considerably widened.

However, there are no ready-made solutions or effective pre-packaged methods.

The problems faced by teachers in some classes are multifaceted and originate outside schools. Their outward symptoms are constantly varied so that fresh solutions are called for each time they are addressed. Anything may be found anywhere, a state of affairs liable to result in demoralization. As the author of the present study writes, 'there is no such thing as a permanently solved problem'. Yet, there is no firmly founded body of theoretical principles or formulas that has really stood the test of time. Hence, it is all the more urgent and essential to consider how future teachers should be best prepared to work in conditions unknown to their elders, and to take on multiple and new roles.

No one was better equipped to guide us in this exercise than Jean-Louis Auduc, *professeur agrégé* in history, who began by discovering this new context on the job in the *collèges* and *lycées* of the Paris suburbs. He then stood back from this direct involvement to organize the introduction of pre-service and in-service teacher training concerning school populations considered difficult, and on conflict management, at the Institut universitaire de formation des maîtres at Créteil.

After emphasizing the radical changes in school intake and in the attitudes towards school of at least some of these new groups of pupils – and, consequently, the urgency of different approaches to preparing future teachers for a challenging profession that – Jean-Louis Auduc reviews the outcome of these trends. He draws attention, first, to the steady increase in the presence of ethnic minorities, and to the democratic need to understand these different cultures, before going on to outline means to consider them as a rich contribution to the preparation and implementation of a common educational strategy.

In the following chapter, he addresses the central problem of the relationship of young people to knowledge, and of its development. He shows how one can and must ensure that these 'new' young people are capable of sound attainment, drawing special attention to different ways of tackling interpersonal problems involving pupils in the classroom, and to education for citizenship through the promotion of essential values such as respect for others. Thus, teachers have to be trained to alternate lessons with the entire class and small group activity, and become fully familiar with the notion of learning in successive stages – training in which the use of new technologies should make a useful contribution.

The author then focuses on those groups that are the furthest removed from school culture and consequently tend to reject it, sometimes violently. He addresses the problems of authority and discipline, and proposes solutions for reducing aggressive behaviour on the part of pupils, by encouraging the development of individual strategies based on an accepted set of rules. He rightly emphasizes the very deep need among the most rebellious young people for a sympathetic hearing, together with the benefits of co-operation between teachers and other support staff both within and outside schools. He also demonstrates the importance of developing positive relations with the families of pupils.

Finally, in chapter V, the author considers teamwork in more detail. He forcefully emphasizes that teamwork has become crucial to teaching, and that curricula should be adapted to the particular circumstances facing each school. In the concluding chapter he summarizes his analysis and the strategies he proposes for teaching in this new context.

To criticize Mr Auduc for failing to provide specific formulas or a detailed review of teaching methods adapted to the reality of 'difficult' classes would be to overlook the fact that such methods do not exist. No country has yet adapted its education system to this profound cultural revolution. The author's major contribution lies in his advice to teachers to help them counter their sense of bewilderment, and in his proposals for new content in teacher training programmes, without denying that solutions have to be found individually on a case-by-case basis, frequently, on the spot.

Jean-Claude Eicher
Associate Editor

Contents

Contents

Introduction

Since the beginning of the 1990s, whether in Europe, Canada, the United States of America or Australia, schools have had to contend with a growth in violence which has become far more widespread and conspicuous than previously. School can no longer be regarded as a place sheltered from the violence of urban communities and the street. These phenomena are emerging at a time when teachers have to confront increasingly diverse groups of pupils who are posing new problems for them as a result of their negative perception of schools. Compulsory schooling has opened up the institution to virtually all children and adolescents, so school has come to play a vital part in the process of social integration. Young people now attend both lower and upper secondary schools in developed countries from disadvantaged environments who, 20 or 30 years ago, would never have been educated beyond primary level.

These children belong to ethnic minorities, immigrant communities or families in which the parents may be unemployed or have either never attended school or have not felt comfortable there. The breakdown of family life, the economic crisis, harsh living conditions, problems of insecurity, delinquency, drug-abuse and violence, combined in many cases with an identity crisis regarding their real roots, make such children vulnerable and often unstable. Yet school is the only structure within which this entire age group comes together. It is thus hit head on by such instability and on a far greater scale than previously.

All studies acknowledge that there is no longer (if indeed there ever has been) a single kind of pupil, but several and all types of pupils have to be taken into account. School has to respond to this challenge at a time when society is obliging it to question its fundamental aims. Indeed, failure at school in a society hit by unemployment and crisis is increasingly considered as social failure that precludes positive integration. Simultaneously, school qualifications are increasingly less likely to be automatic passports to employment. This reality reinforces the doubts families may have about school, as huge numbers of young people in *lycées* (upper-secondary schools or their equivalent) reach attainment levels unknown to their parents who, no doubt, never expected to see them achieve such results.

The point at issue is therefore how to deal with those young people from disadvantaged environments, who in no way share the school's goals. How is one to approach those described by a senior French Ministry of Education official in 1995 as socially illiterate and scholastically anorexic, given their lack of a reference system enabling them to adapt to society, as well as their conflictual relations with school?

Confronted with this situation, most developed countries, regardless of the organization of their education system, began to respond in the early 1970s. The approaches developed included the following:

- positive discrimination measures in the form of additional posts, and teaching time and equipment for schools with an intake felt to be difficult. While the criteria here have varied with the country concerned, they generally take account of family incomes, the presence of pupils from ethnic minorities, run-down residential conditions, and petty offences or criminality in or around the school;
- the development of study options (learning the community languages other than the dominant language of instruction, technology, etc.) considered more appropriate to the expectations and needs of pupils and their families;
- the establishment around the school of broader social support measures, in liaison with local authorities and their social services, as well as the police and judicial authorities.

While all such initiatives are of unquestionable value, in that they can help prevent material damage, and violence among pupils, they do not face up to the question of how to improve the relationship young people have with school, so that they benefit fully from what is taught. The response to this question requires reconsideration of the real nature of teaching, as well as the transmission of knowledge and the preparation of teachers who work with a very diverse school population.

The different strategies which have been attempted in schools may be put into two categories: those based on an analysis of difficulties linked to the environment outside the school (such as unemployment, family problems and living conditions); and those deriving from an analysis of shortcomings in the way pupils relate to school, to knowledge and its different levels of knowledge, to learning activity, different forms of school work, and so forth.

As regards the first category, the extent to which action within the school can tackle these 'difficulties' appears limited, an impression that very often fuels pessimism or even a disconcerting fatalism.

As to the second, consideration of the professional aspects of getting to grips with such problems is possible, even though substantial human and financial investment may be required to keep pace with a very real deterioration in conditions outside the school. Pre-service training can address these problems, in particular through analysis and exchange of information on methods and practice currently employed in the field. The aim must be to encourage discussion of such practice during pre-service training and try to clarify it, so that schools and classrooms are more understandable to new teachers.

For a very long time, pre-service teacher training was based on techniques for passing on knowledge including, to a variable extent from one country to the next, some understanding of child psychology, knowledge of the pupil, and teaching methods. The older the pupils concerned, particularly in upper secondary education, the more teacher training gave priority to the 'transmission of knowledge' aspect, rather than aspects of teaching practice as such. Yet it is primarily in lower and upper secondary education, in the 12-16 age group, that the alienation and difficulties experienced by young people vis-à-vis school are most evident. Furthermore, there is an enormous disparity between how teachers experienced their own schooling as former pupils and the daily experience, in both the classroom and life itself, of pupils in some institutions catering for disadvantaged communities, who increasingly question the very meaning of school.

Confrontation at school with disadvantaged pupils puts the identity and practice of teachers severely to the test. It can result in rejection or positive interest. Faced with a growing number of expectations, responsibilities and tasks, teachers frequently have the impression that the content of their occupation has become blurred. Often, they conclude that the difficulties of pupils are attributable to the fact that school and learning have lost any meaning for them, and question the development of activities related to their teaching duties in the classroom. The idea that the solution to difficulty with school is not to be found in a didactic approach to subject-based knowledge in the classroom, is reinforced. Yet the research carried out (Charlot, et al., 1993) shows that where work on the acquisition of knowledge is discontinued, school attainment suffers; and that teaching methods dictated solely by professional considerations, or pupil performance, prevents them from developing an appreciation of content for its own sake and exposes them to failure.

In any event, these new difficulties support the case for teachers undergoing training that involves specific preparation, in particular for the following critical areas:

- social distance vis-à-vis the working environment, and cultural confrontation with the school population;
- integration within an institutional team;
- non-stigmatization of schools and emphasis on achievements;
- managing the temporal aspect: in schools considered difficult, there is no such thing as a permanently solved problem; situations are always on the brink of breakdown, which will occur unless there is constant vigilance.

Specific training for those who are to teach pupils considered difficult does not mean that teaching should become an entirely different occupation. But it does mean that teachers who work with these pupils should possess qualities and aptitudes that can be readily mobilized in all schools. Indeed, problems encountered with such groups and the means to solving them are not peripheral to the system. They are intrinsic to the way change is occurring and are magnified to reveal more explicitly difficulties which are discreetly omnipresent elsewhere.

The aim should be to identify the features of a particular kind of training which puts a premium on analysis, and encourages discussion of methods and practice actually implemented on the job. Such training is vital, since schools with a difficult pupil intake, can generate personal or professional situations which make teaching in them, if not a 'high-risk' occupation, at least one from which 'crisis' or 'stress' are rarely absent. Teachers of the pupils concerned are prompted to question themselves more frequently than elsewhere, about themselves, their methods, the pupils, the environment and the future. These and similar considerations can be professionally disturbing for some while, for others, they can drive a process of change within the education system. And they can also lead to situations of unhappiness and revulsion or, alternatively, to remarkably rapid progress in skills development.

Regardless of the extent to which their education systems are centralized, very many countries are faced with the need to provide teacher training capable of dealing with violent situations at school, and each of them must consider how best to deliver it. The problem is of no less concern to developing countries, in which young people have to attend school for much longer than previously. Such young people, who are the first to attend school within their families and often go out to work for a small wage, pose problems for school institutions that traditional teaching methods are powerless to address.

Training aimed at adapting teachers to classroom realities and the differences between pupils is the only way of ensuring that the former play a leading role in the education system and plan their teaching creatively. It means practical teacher preparation for work with others, rather than carrying out their activities alone. The obligation to work in a team is more than just a legal provision: it is an essential precondition for the conduct of teaching, one of its basic occupational aspects. While teachers may be alone in the classroom, they should not manage and undergo difficulties in isolation. For this reason, the concept of a network has to be developed. Within schools, all mature teaching and administrative staff should act together to assist pupils, in ways dictated by their individual duties and responsibilities. Teamwork is easier because these different occupations complement each other. And its overriding aim must be to provide pupils with a common consistent perspective, while enabling members of the team to communicate and respond rapidly among themselves.

Pre-service teacher training should also enable them to develop a partnership with all those involved in the educational process. They have to be shown how to identify the contact and resource persons who may become partners and support their activities, within the local environment of the school. They should also learn to consider the support they may be able to offer such partners in return.

Depending on different countries and schools, these partners may be attached to various institutions:

- educational support staff, such as child psychologists or guidance counsellors;
- local authorities employing special trainers, social welfare workers, etc.;
- community groups offer trainers and educators in the arts, cultural activities or sports;
- services such as the police or judicial authorities.

Partnerships must also be open to families or their representatives. A substantial part of the training programme should focus on the kind of relations that teachers wish to develop with them.

Finally, although the task of managing the situation in neighbourhoods considered difficult is certainly one for a team including teachers and other members of the education system, it should also involve all social agencies active in these neighbourhoods. Thus teacher training should unquestionably include joint training with the other persons involved. Irrespective of their responsibilities, status, qualifications, or the purpose and content of their professional duties, all those who work in neighbourhoods where communities are disadvantaged, have a certain number of activities in common, including contact with culturally different groups, and decisions relating to people in difficulty. The electricity company official who cuts off the supply to a family unable to pay as a result of unemployment, the teacher who has to give marks to pupils unable to work at home because of living conditions there, the police officer and magistrate who arrest and try young mothers for theft – should not all such persons be committed to joint consideration of their working methods, their responsibilities and, in the final analysis, the meaning of their occupations?

The foregoing points all demonstrate the importance of multidimensional teacher training. The challenges involved are quite clearly as follows:

- preparing future teachers for their occupation in expectation of a wide variety of responsibilities and tasks;
- giving them a foundation which, in conjunction with subsequent training adapted to the reality of their school, will enable them to be as effective working with pupils considered difficult, as with those from more privileged social backgrounds;
- making them actively aware of their occupation and its purpose: mounting a wholesale drive to ensure that no young people, whatever their origin, are left by the wayside and that all can develop their individual potential.

I. Teaching in schools or classes considered difficult: a contemporary challenge

The question of teaching in schools or classes considered difficult has assumed increased significance in developed countries in recent years.

Changes in the school population

The teaching of difficult pupils only really assumes crucial importance once society entrusts school with the responsibility for an entire age group, and expects the school system to adequately serve all pupils. Once the needs of a country dictate that no pupil can be left by the wayside, the education system has to be concerned with the schooling of all young people regardless of where they live, or their ethnic or social origins. School, therefore, has a responsibility to encourage all pupils' maximum attainment, and not just the very small proportion closest to its norms.

The schooling of an entire age group, or the great majority of it, moves the debate into the whole area of problems such as intercultural relations or immigration. It results in school being viewed not simply as a centre for the transmission of knowledge, but as a place for socialization, which in turn implies that actors in the education system should be concerned with questions regarding the prevention of delinquency or aggressive forms of behaviour.

In several countries, one of the responsibilities of school is to prevent social unrest in certain neighbourhoods. This kind of strategy leads countries, such as France or the USA, to adopt similar solutions without it always being possible to know whether these approaches have reciprocally influenced each other, or are a coincidence. France has its difficult suburbs, the USA its run-down inner urban areas. In order to fight exclusion, insecurity or drugs, both often analyze the role of school in identical ways. Lynn Curtis, Director General of the

Milton Eisenhower Foundation in Washington, which specializes in urban and social issues, describes what works: "schooling from the earliest age, the creation of 'peaceful havens' for doing homework after school, the appointment of mentors for the oldest pupils, all such educational initiatives are the most successful....." (*Le Point*, 11 May 1996).

In France, the creation of educational priority areas (ZEPs, or *zones d'éducation prioritaires*) mainly comprising primary schools, lower-secondary schools known as *collèges*, and a few *lycées* or upper-secondary schools, along with the classification of institutions catering for the 11-15 age group (at *collèges*) or the 15-18 age group (at *lycées*) into the 'sensitive' category, have enabled some of these schools to secure additional staff resources. The same institutions have also developed links with the local social and cultural environment, particularly through the development of *school support services* to help pupils from disadvantaged backgrounds to do their homework.

Recent changes have altered the social landscape

Recently, changes have led to alterations in the general context of the teaching profession and the field in which it operates, as follows:

- increase in the number of pupils in secondary education;
- a more diversified school population;
- the introduction of new streams within schools;
- the patent emergence of a set of social – as opposed to exclusively school-related – problems in institutions for 12-18-year-olds. Comprehensive schools for all pupils up to the age of 15 or 16, as in most European countries, have resulted in formerly separate categories of pupils being brought into extensive regular contact with each other.

By becoming more democratic, the education system is now catering for pupils of very varied sociocultural origin and levels of attainment. These circumstances call for teaching methods different from those formerly used in much more homogeneous classes of children, most of whom received sound family support.

"The multicultural dimension of society is bringing with it new challenges. Whereas school has to adapt increasingly to the local context, society itself is diversifying (...). Teachers must therefore acquire fresh understanding, so that they have a better grasp of the social context of education, and are better equipped to deal with conflict and to explain or defend specific teaching solutions." (Council of Europe, 1987).

Teaching has to adapt

In the space of a few years, we have moved from a situation in which pupils had, or were supposed, to adapt to teaching, to one in which teaching now has to adapt to pupils. Since 1995, Italian, French, Swedish and Spanish school curricula have all strongly emphasized the need to individualize teaching. The same situation is to be found in developing countries, as testified by a teacher from Bombay (India) referring to the schooling of children in shantytown suburbs: "Teaching methods and the curriculum are totally unsuited to the living conditions and culture of these children. If we want them to be able to study, they should have a properly adapted system"[1].

The notion of school failure was strongly highlighted in the 1970s to explain difficulties in teaching. In this context, the need was for teachers to take account of pupils' different paces of learning. In the 1990s, violence, within or outside schools, receives priority attention when teaching difficulties are debated. This shift is neither lacking in significance, nor unrelated to the development of the social exclusion which exists in some neighbourhoods. For public opinion in some Western European countries, this shift implies that schools which enrol very large numbers of pupils with educational difficulties and which, in the 1970s and 1980s, appeared to constitute centres of innovation in teaching practice, have today become crisis institutions in urban areas regarded as dangerous.

1.   *Famille et Éducation*, No. 404, December 1996.

Schools now bear the brunt of frustration and contradictions in society

The social fabric and mechanisms responsible for the construction and breakdown of group identity, problems of delinquency and racism, processes of exclusion and segregation, and the capacity of towns and cities to function in the interests of integration, have become central concerns in all industrialized countries. And they are also those of today's schools which, while they may be special places for the social integration of all young people, are also places in which exclusion may first be experienced in concrete form. Today, school itself brings social frustration and contradictions into sharp focus. After carrying forward the aspirations of the greatest number, it now appears as a place where success may contribute to social advancement but is not guaranteed and in which social rifts are becoming increasingly self-evident.

In addition, school as a social institution has gradually assumed responsibilities formerly the preserve of other institutions that have today declined in influence or are undergoing change. For example, the family has greatly altered in the last half-century, so that school is the only well-ordered place with which many children are familiar.

The deterioration in the environment of some schools

Schools directly suffer the consequences of the deterioration in living conditions of their surrounding communities. Educational staff have both to take account of the reality of such situations and, at the same time, establish a margin for manoeuvre to carry out their duties[2]. They therefore have to analyze exactly what is happening in their environment and, in particular, the deterioration in the local situation of the most disadvantaged categories experienced in recent years in most developed countries, especially in certain areas of major cities.

Indeed, it is clear – though without any implied stigmatization – that phenomena associated with the deterioration in housing conditions,

2.   See Chapter IV, p. 82, *Schools are not a mirror image of circumstances outside them*

increased unemployment, and the growth of delinquency and, in particular, of drug trafficking, mainly afflict the residents of certain neighbourhoods. Such phenomena have major repercussions for schools, which are reflected in negative attitudes on the part of pupils regarding the aims of school and, more tangibly, by marked absenteeism and aggressive forms of behaviour.

All such neighbourhood problems are supplemented by an over-accumulation of personal difficulties in integrating within societies affected by crisis – difficulties suffered by young people in recently settled immigrant families from the former colonies of Western European countries in particular. In this case, the problems of cultural diversity and mastery of the language are experienced alongside the social problems of communities in neighbourhoods where disadvantaged groups are concentrated.

At the end of 1994, an official report of the French Ministry of Education described the socio-economic environment of certain school institutions as follows: "sometimes extreme precariousness characterized by economic, social, cultural and emotional poverty. And the first victims of this lack of affection are the children who, from the earliest age, suffer the anxieties of their parents (...) These precarious circumstances are further aggravated by the housing conditions not to mention noise and indiscriminate overcrowding (...) In some areas, unemployment reaches 35-40 per cent. These anxieties and the tension resulting from them give rise to commonplace, mundane violence. School failure often felt to be natural enough by families and children is the result of a lack of motivation, and the inability of parents to help their children or, indeed, to control them. (...) Numerous French single-parent families are herded together in difficult areas, where rents are lowest. Children there are often left to their own devices, not to say ignored or even abandoned (...); school alone will not manage to re-motivate them by giving them some hope of a decent life (...) Underachievement at school of immigrant children and adolescents leads them into a sort of resignation or despair, making them vulnerable to religious extremists. (...) In such cases, therefore, school institutions are located in the middle of real ghettos: ghettos of economic precariousness, of foreign cultures and of rejection of school. Considerable and sometimes long-term absenteeism is generally supplemented by serious mental anguish giving rise to the indiscriminate consumption of tranquillizers, withdrawal, depression and even suicide" (Braustein, Dasté, 1994, pp. 13-15).

The development of compensatory education policies: giving more to those who have less

In this environment characteristic of many cities in western Europe and North America, school, despite its shortcomings, remains the best agency for integrating and developing the social awareness of young people, even though it is also often the first stage in social exclusion and social reproduction (the perpetuation of social stratification). Within this context, it is crucial to reinvest all such young people who have become violent through desperation, with the sense of a worthwhile future, confidence, hope and motivation.

Yet schooling for all is very expensive. In the financial crises affecting some countries, budgets earmarked for education have levelled out or even been cut back. However, it would today seem that the educational sector is becoming a priority for educational decision-makers. One recalls the words of the President of Harvard, Derek Bok: "If you think education is expensive, try ignorance".

Most governments in this situation have chosen to try and compensate for the difficulties of these pupils by increasing the resources of the schools which enrol them. This is the policy of 'giving more to those who have less'.

The supplementary resources policy in the Netherlands

In the **Netherlands**, there is a system of 'supplementary resources' for certain categories of pupils. These compensatory 'enrichment' resources are intended for pupils from disadvantaged environments and children from immigrant families. The budget of each school is raised in proportion to the number of children from disadvantaged or immigrant families for which it caters. While the coefficient for an 'average' child is 1, the coefficient for a working-class child is 1.25 and, for a child of immigrant origin, 1.9. The additional funding is for setting up smaller classes, remedial classes study groups, or special assistance with homework.

In the Netherlands, 90 formally identified urban areas displaying numerous social problems, such as unemployment and poor housing conditions, are mainly concentrated in the four cities of Rotterdam, Amsterdam, Utrecht and The Hague. Schools in these areas receive special funding from the Ministry of Education to support collaboration between them and social welfare agencies. This supplementary resources policy has led to the development of smaller class size, and remedial resources that promote educational attainment for children who accept school values but require more individualized assistance to achieve better results.

However, this compensatory policy has run into various problems. The existence of several kinds of schooling in the Netherlands has led to the concentration of pupils in difficulty in certain institutions, with the development of hostility to school and absenteeism. Furthermore, for many pupils, the problem is not merely one of underachievement, but that school and school-based knowledge have lost any meaning for them. They make no real effort in their schoolwork. Finally, the result of increased unemployment in certain areas is that young people who have never seen their parents at work, fail to appreciate the need for qualifications in order to secure a footing on the labour market.

Initiatives to develop jobs in the areas concerned have been launched to complement the 'supplementary resources' policy, so that pupils become more motivated towards schooling. In this context, schemes introduced jointly by local authorities and schools need to be evaluated for their impact on pupil attainment and their access to skilled jobs.

The ZEPs and 'sensitive' school institutions in France

In **France**, the educational priority areas (ZEPs) were created in 1982. In 1996, they comprised 1,300,000 pupils in 544 schools (primary schools, *collèges* and *lycées*, particularly vocational *lycées*) whose catchment areas pose especially acute social problems and where school achievement indicators point to particularly weak performance. This system was supplemented in 1992 and 1993 by the classification of 167 lower- and upper-secondary schools (*collèges* and *lycées*) as 'sensitive', mainly because of the violence they were liable to encounter.

These ZEP or 'sensitive' institutions benefit from supplementary resources unavailable to other schools. They include budgetary allocations, teaching posts, guidance, social or health staff, and the allocation to them of young people for supervisory duties during their periods of national service. Staff working in them receive specific allowances and career bonuses.

Systems of 'compensatory education' or 'positive discrimination' in other countries

In the **French Community of Belgium**, where failure and drop-out are also a serious problem, educational priority areas have been similarly introduced.

In the **Flemish Community of Belgium**, priority education has operated since the start of the 1991 school year. To guide those working in the urban areas concerned, 26 teaching posts have been created. A Flemish Fund for the Integration of the Disadvantaged (VFIK) has been set up.

The **United Kingdom** had set up its own Educational Priority Areas as schemes for schools intending to apply positive discrimination in certain urban areas, following publication of the Plowden Report (1967). The Low Attainments Pupils Programme (LAPP) was introduced in England during the 1990s.

Systems based on similar principles exist in secondary education elsewhere, as in **Spain**, **Denmark** and **Quebec**.

In **Portugal**, the education minister has also established an Educational Priority Area. His **Greek** counterpart, meanwhile, is working on the definitions and appropriate measures for 'Urban Areas at Risk'.

While such policies making it possible to reduce class size and allocate additional educational resources have been successful in certain cases, their impact remains limited, as a result of difficulties encountered by teachers in working with these new groups of pupils. Stress can be lessened by helping teachers and pupils to coexist more comfortably in one and the same place. Yet getting to the root of these matters implies a closer examination of school and classroom practice. Knowledge and learning are permanent dimensions of the classroom and of education. Work on learning content, on methods and on the use of additional resources, therefore, all have to be co-ordinated for pupils to achieve sound results.

"Fatiha, a reasonable pupil, feels that it is normal enough to learn about one's past for one, two, or three hours a year, but to do so for an entire year is sickening. So the history teacher can do what he likes, using traditional methods or group work, or teach standing on his head – anything he fancies to get things going – but he won't succeed if the teaching method is not considered alongside the question of what sense it makes, to Fatiha, to attend something called a history lesson" (Charlot, 1997).

If teachers do not start to think about the meaning of learning and the importance to pupils of being present, the essential additional resources for compensating for their difficulties will not enable them to develop overall personal goals, along with the desire to learn and possess knowledge.

Preparing teachers for classroom reality

A vicious circle common to numerous countries has been observed, namely that schools enrolling those regarded as the most difficult pupils are often assigned the least experienced teachers who have to win their spurs on the most depressing of battlegrounds. This situation has persisted notwithstanding the financial incentives offered in some countries.

Qualitative research by American sociologists and ethnologists showed that white teachers working in schools attended by African-American children were only barely familiar with their way of life. An irreparable divide seems to separate teachers who live in comfortable residential suburbs and earn enough to be tax payers, and their pupils whose families as a rule are at or below the poverty line, excluding them from income taxation, and live in run-down neighbourhoods. The great majority of such teachers are keen to get away fast from these schools to which they have been posted at the start of their careers against their will, and have an extremely negative image of residents and the parents of pupils (Ogbu, 1974; Rosenfeld, 1971).

Research conducted in France in the 1990s has revealed, in a way somewhat similar to that of the USA in 1970, a rift between the private world of middle-class teachers and that of their working-class pupils and their parents. This separation between pupils from disadvantaged backgrounds and education professionals who find it increasingly difficult to tolerate their working conditions is especially noticeable in the lower-secondary schools or *collèges*, and is becoming increasingly so in primary schools (Debarbieux, 1996).

It is thus vital to address such questions fully in the pre-service training, so that beginning teachers are equipped to confront these situations when they start work. Numerous problems include the following:

- authority in the classroom;
- learning about socialization, at the same time as subject-based knowledge;
- forestalling high-risk behaviour;
- fighting school failure;
- difficulty in providing remedial help outside the classroom.

How are teachers to enable young people from disadvantaged backgrounds to secure access to the right information, at an acceptable educational level, while remaining attached to the environment in which they live? This is the challenge facing schools in all modern societies. Proposed responses differ depending on the country:

- co-ordinating school activities with other urban services;
- making animators and youth workers available;
- management of very large classes;
- determining whether the most disadvantaged pupils can be taught a minimum amount, and still be able to study to higher levels;
- identifying what is most helpful for those who progress least.

Over and above the question of content, therefore, all schools have to make it possible for pupils to learn how to learn.

The apprehensiveness of first-time teachers

Teachers at lower- and upper-secondary schools often start their first assignment with many preconceptions – built around media images, apprehensions, fear or sometimes deeper anxiety associated with the climate and environment of their school. They do so in an age when the public image of school is no longer what it was. In the developed countries a few decades back, school still had a determinant part to play in equipping children for life in society. Teachers held authority and dispensed knowledge. They had before them pupils equal before the law, who had to follow a model and receive lessons. The moral, intellectual and social authority of the school extended well beyond its walls. In this respect, teachers nowadays may think they have nothing left, least of all their social position, their monopoly of the transmission of knowledge and their authority.

The situation may be summed up in one of the slogans chanted by 18-year-old French *lycée* students in various strikes and marches: With the *bac*' (short for *baccalauréat*, the secondary school leaving certificate), 'you have nothing; without it, you are nothing'. This slogan applicable to the school context in numerous countries, means:

- young people with a school education alone can no longer count on a job with certainty;
- without such education, a young person is sure to become socially marginalized.

A sense of 'shock' for beginners

The discovery that school is attended by many new kinds of pupil is something of a 'shock' to most first-time teachers. From surveys of new teachers conducted in the eastern suburbs of Paris, the main difficulty referred to clearly concerns the listening problems of pupils. Whereas during their initial training, these teachers thought that learning essentially meant listening, they have now discovered that what counts above all is to motivate pupils to listen to them (Davisse; Rochex, 1995).

One beneficial outcome of a 'cultural shock' of this kind can be to help teachers realize that what they thought was a universal conception of school and culture is, sociologically, only their own. Yet most frequently the results are mental resignation, escapism, insecurity and low morale on the part of staff, instead of stable motivated teachers who can enable young people to do well in these disadvantaged areas.

Teachers confronted with pupils who are difficult or unwilling to learn, naturally have to reconsider what teaching involves, as well as their conception of what it means to be a pupil or teacher, and the meaning of school and its role within society:

- Educating (well-being/relationships);
- Teaching (learning and knowledge);
- Training (know-how/skills).

Teachers – a fairly young professional group

In France, teachers assigned to schools with a difficult pupil intake are typically younger, less experienced and less committed to remain in their assigned schools than other professional categories. The same phenomenon is readily observable in all developed countries.

At the same time, the ageing of teaching staff in Western Europe is becoming increasingly self-evident. The average age of teachers in the Netherlands is over 40; in Denmark, over 50 per cent of teachers are older than 38; in the German *Hauptschulen*, 60 per cent are over 40. In France, half of practising teachers are aged between 42 and 50. In many countries, therefore, a major intake of new teachers is to be expected in the next 10-15 years, putting the training issue very firmly on the agenda. In France, for example, the intense recruitment of the 1990s, leading to a relative standstill between 1997 and around 2003, will then pick up strongly as the 'baby boom' generation reaches retirement age. This was recognized back in 1987 by the 15th session of the Permanent Conference of European Ministers of Education enlarged to include those of Canada, Japan and theUSA.

"The mass of teachers recruited in the 1960s and 1970s in response to the growth in school enrolments have reached – or are approaching – the middle of their careers. It is thus becoming urgent to adapt the knowledge, skills and attitudes of an ageing profession to rapidly evolving needs. The pressures resulting from these trends are bringing with them fresh challenges for teachers as educational professionals." (Council of Europe, 1987).

Training more geared to the specific needs of new teachers

In recent years, teacher training in the developed countries has gradually ceased to be organized in terms of an occupation whose basic task is to transmit knowledge, developing instead the idea that teaching also means the organization of situations in which learning occurs. Training has sought to be better adapted to the specific needs of pupils, to exploit the academic knowledge of psychology and sociology in methods analysis, and to take account of the fact that people do not learn by listening to speeches, but by acting.

Preparing teachers for their occupation

The idea that teaching is increasingly perceived as **praxis**, in which the teacher organizes situations conducive to skills development on the part of pupils themselves has been at the heart of reforms in teacher training curricula. Such developments have not always been straightforward, as evidenced by the debate in France over the creation of the *Instituts Universitaires de Formation des Maîtres* (IUFM) or University Institutes for Teacher Training, which some felt laid too much emphasis on problems of teaching per se at the expense of subject-based knowledge.

"Compulsory secondary education has very rarely had the staff it needed to tackle its inevitable difficulties under better circumstances" according to Leclercq (1993, p. 109). Most teacher training in Western Europe occurs either in university or, alternatively, in professional institutes with courses related to both academic content and teaching practice (see *Table 1*).

Table 1.   Pre-service teacher training in Europe

	Pre-school	**Primary**	**Lower secondary**	**Upper secondary**
Belgium	Non-university	Non-university	Non-university	University
Denmark	Non-university	Non-university	Non-university	University
Germany	Non-university	University	University	University
Greece	University	University	University	University
Spain	University	University	University	University
France	University	University	University	University
Ireland	Non-university	University	University	University
Italy	Non-university	Non-university	Non-university	University
Luxembourg	Non-university	Non-university	University	University
The Netherlands	Non-university	Non-university	Non-university	University
Portugal	Non-university	Non-university	University	University
United Kingdom	University	University	University	University

EURYDICE, *Measures to combat failure at school: a challenge for the construction of Europe (summary analysis),* p. 15, November 1993.

The idea is that teachers should have both a sound academic preparation to satisfy curricular requirements, together with a good grounding in teaching skills to meet pupil needs and, as a result, be better placed to respond to classroom diversity. One of the most frequent concerns of teacher trainers is to ensure that courses are as close as possible to real teaching conditions.

Preparing teachers to be organizers of learning situations

Teachers must be able to create and organize situations conducive to learning. While this should mean they are capable of adapting to different kinds of pupils, the training issue becomes that much more complex. As Walker (1992) stated in a report to the Council of Europe, "we often expect teachers to know automatically how to handle delicate situations, even though this is not a part of their official training".

In certain countries, the first sign of awareness that specific training has to be developed for teaching these difficult groups has been in in-service training programmes. The latter have often approached the issue by focusing on the problems of recent young immigrant arrivals in mastering language (for example, the network of teaching counsellors in Belgium, Denmark and Germany, or the CEFISEM, the information and training centres for the schooling of children of migrants, in France). In all cases, training occurred subsequent to practical experience of diversity.

The need to replenish teaching staff in all developed countries, together with the fact that the situation of disadvantaged communities, while still only affecting a minority, is an increasingly less marginal phenomenon, have meant that preparation for work with difficult groups of pupils has become an unavoidable issue in pre-service training.

Teachers cannot be transformed into youth leaders, social workers, police officers or judges. They do need to be prepared, however, for all aspects of their occupation and classroom activity, including its violence, so that their teaching is as effective as possible. Once the question of teaching in schools in difficult areas is viewed in terms of incentive, voluntary commitment and specific bonuses, that of organizing the training follows quite naturally.

Necessary advance training

In some countries, ministries have firmly decided not to assign any first-time teacher to difficult schools. But besides the fact that this solution is hard to put into practice, it only shifts the problem, since the difficulties already referred to and, in particular, the phenomena associated with violence also affect some classes in institutions regarded as normal. Training adapted to such problems is thus essential. The teachers, for their part, are highly apprehensive about having to confront these difficulties and, as a result, are strongly in favour of practical training. The upshot for the practice of teaching in difficult institutions is the need for a move from training after this experience, to prior training aimed at preparing future teachers to adapt to all situations they might encounter during their careers.

All surveys conducted in recent years in Belgium, France, the USA, Switzerland and Quebec indicate that teachers find their pre-service training too theoretical and not practical enough (Dupuy-Walker, 1990). In particular, they find it inadequate in terms of real classroom experience, especially as regards problems of discipline, pupil motivation, class management and their relations with pupils.

In Australia, a study by D. S. Anderson (1974) showed that teachers who are attracted primarily to their occupation out of interest in their subject, the opportunity for contact with young people and passing on knowledge, are the practitioners who – in comparison with those from other professions, such as legal experts, engineers and doctors – are the least confident about how to define their role, even after completing some initial training. The same conclusions are to be found in a 1992 survey conducted by the Direction de l'Évaluation et de la Prospective (Department of Evaluation and Planning) of the French Ministry of Education, on French teachers nominated to a ZEP for their initial posting, in 1991-92.

- Of those teachers assigned to a ZEP ,express their disappointment or disillusion in relation to their initial conception of their occupation.
- A total of 51 per cent consider the school in general to be 'less than moderately', 'insignificantly' or 'not at all' pleasant.

As to the difficulties encountered during their first year, the same teachers emphasize the following:

- for 27 per cent, problems of demotivation, absenteeism and lack of discipline among pupils;
- for 25 per cent, very mixed-ability classes and low pupil performance;
- for 19 per cent, problems relating to social difficulties, and abdication of responsibility by parents;
- for 11 per cent, difficulties in communicating knowledge to pupils and motivating them.

It is clear that, henceforth, the dimension of 'teaching difficult groups of pupils' has necessarily to be included in the pre-service training of teachers. Besides aspects concerned with the educational aptitudes of those being taught, teachers posted in ZEPs experience specific difficulties attributable to the behaviour of pupils and their social and family environment. What teachers term the 'abdication' of parents, an aspect to be qualified in the chapters that follow, is reflected in lack of motivation, absenteeism and absence of discipline on the part of pupils. Because they are insufficiently prepared for such difficulties, around 40 per cent of teachers whose first appointment is in a ZEP think they will give up teaching in public education. Training is all the more crucial in that underlying the difficulties experienced by teachers are the following considerations:

- knowledge acquisition is very closely linked to the question of employment, and young people from disadvantaged environments are increasingly aware of the fact;
- schools, *collèges* and *lycées* catering for young people with educational and social difficulties are, as a whole, places where changes are being experienced increasingly fast. These institutions are not solely places where teachers 'suffer' but, by

the same token and out of necessity, an arena for positive transformations in professional practice.

In several countries, training courses for teaching difficult groups of pupils and for handling violent situations in schools have been established. They aim to explain to would-be teachers that, while certain elements are essential for work in difficult classes or institutions, they are useful everywhere. The concerns of the courses are as follows:

• to inform trainees about what must be avoided at all costs in such schools, in order to be able to teach there;
• to give them assurance and confidence in the field of subject-based knowledge, as well as that of familiarity with the groups they will teach, and their backgrounds;
• to prevent first-time teachers from working entirely on their own, and encourage their integration into a school or district team.

Courses of this kind belong to a professional training approach seeking to ensure that, throughout their careers, teachers will be able to adapt to a variety of different institutions and update their professional skills.

II. Making teachers aware of the characteristics of schools regarded as difficult

The cultural background of most teachers in schools regarded as difficult is far removed from that of their pupils. It is therefore important that they should be aware of the characteristics of the groups of pupils who attend these institutions – including the existence of communities from minority immigrant or ethnic backgrounds, and difficult living conditions, etc. – and led to consider ways of taking the social, ethnic, religious and cultural diversity of pupils into account. One problem is that, while the intake of schools considered difficult is up to a point homogeneous as regards the social circumstances of pupils (such as their living conditions, family unemployment, etc.), the latter nevertheless come from very diverse backgrounds. These differences are numerous and striking. They include the length of time immigrant communities have been settled in the host country, the scale and nature of the migrations concerned, the national and civic status of immigrants, the development of their communities, and their position vis-à-vis the public authorities. Analysis of the schooling of children from 'immigrant' or 'minority' groups thus reflects differences between their societies of origin regarding the conception of relations between state and nation, and of the part to be played by the school in processes of national integration.

In the USA and the United Kingdom, the term 'minorities' is used to refer to groups identified not only in terms of their origin and culture but, often, also by virtue of the fact they possess so-called 'second-class citizenship'. In France, the term 'minority' is strongly controversial, if not out of order, since it challenges the rhetoric and practical effectiveness of republicanism. The educational policies of the last 30 years in the English-speaking countries clearly demonstrate a shift from a strongly nationalist perspective based on the idea of assimilation, to both a relativist multicultural position sensitive to the specific features of each culture, and an anti-racist approach directed at structural inequalities and different kinds of oppression. These trends are indicative of changes in people's conception of the role of society, as well as the position within it of ethnic and racial minorities, and also social and economic changes in the countries under consideration.

The schooling of young people from an immigrant background in France

The establishment of compensatory measures on an area basis apparently takes little account of the cultural and ethnic origin of children. Yet although these arrangements are theoretically targeted at all pupils from disadvantaged backgrounds, they are usually applied to those from an immigrant background (Payet, 1989, 1994).

A report to the Conseil Économique et Social (Economic and Social Council) in June 1994 showed that, in France, very little attention is paid to national origin in analyzing pupil performance. The latter depends, above all, on socio-economic level, the size of the family and the attitude of parents vis-à-vis school.

The French education system enrols around a million foreign pupils (8 per cent of the total number of pupils), the great majority of whom attend public schools. For each given socio-economic level, foreign pupils emerge quite favourably from comparisons of performance at school measured in national evaluations conducted at various levels of the education system. School failure is more widespread among pupils who have recently settled in France, or whose schooling in the French system has been repeatedly interrupted by regular return visits to the country of origin (Vallet and Caille, 1996). But the ready involvement of families in the schooling of their children appears determinant in this study. It takes the form of constant interest and participation in pupil guidance, reflecting greater expectations and ambition regarding their children's future.

The expressions 'foreign pupils', or 'pupils of immigrant origin', cover a very wide range of different statuses and school backgrounds. Young people of immigrant stock belong to a diversity of backgrounds on which it is impossible to pin a single label. Each pupil differs from others in terms of his or her individual experience or personality.

Under these circumstances, teachers have to 'prepare themselves in advance to be aware of their own conceptions, attitudes and behaviour in relating to pupils of immigrant origin, in order that communication with them is entirely geared to the provision of effective support' (Clément; Girardin, 1997). Teacher training should therefore cover the complexity of the problems posed by these pupils, and the need for co-operation with all categories of school staff and other partners, including parents, associations, social workers, auxiliary staff and local authorities. Teachers should be provided with the means for:

- understanding the diversity of cultures;

- learning to interpret forms of behaviour;

- becoming familiar with the values and moral code of these young people with regard to matters such as solidarity, honesty, work, and the concept of punishment;

- understanding the family environment and expectations;

- acquiring information about the family life of young people, the urban environment, and the origin of compensatory behaviour patterns or those indicative of maladjustment;

- establishing firm bearings and indicators enabling them to communicate better.

The schooling of young people from ethnic minorities in the USA and the United Kingdom

The United States

Until the 1960s, American schools were conceived of as the melting-pot for the emergence of a new civilization fuelled, in particular, by the transmission at school of a mythical history and culture driven by the English-speaking world which took little account of the American Indian (Native Americans) or African-American contributions, or the influence of more recent immigrants (Body-Gendrot, 1991).

The social movements in the early 1970s led to different types of integration policies:

- school integration of African-American and White children within the same schools;
- an increase in the decision-making power of parents in schools;
- the introduction of positive discrimination measures (policies entailing quotas and preferential treatment).

The researchers most involved in the fight against ethnic or racial inequality have expressed a preference for action aimed at providing pupils themselves with the critical capacity and skills necessary to assume personal responsibility for their own schooling (Delgado-Gaitan and Trueba, 1991).

Statistical analyses regarding inequalities in education are complex. It would appear that (European, Asian, or Latin American) immigrant minorities, the majority of which comprise people who have freely chosen to leave their native countries, do better than minorities which have been, as it were, incorporated against their will into American society (including African-Americans, Hispanics, American Indians [Native Americans] and Puerto Ricans) (Ogbu, 1978, 1987). The most common explanations of difficulties at school faced by the children of minority groups are their low self-esteem due to interiorization of stereotypes about them. A 1990 research project showed that school achievement was closely linked to the opinions expressed by teachers on working habits (including classroom participation, discipline and homework). The finding appears to come out firmly in favour of children of Asian origin who scored highest in this respect, while African-American children were rated far more negatively (Farkas et al., 1990).

The United Kingdom

The arrival in very large numbers of workers from the Commonwealth with their families in the 1960s, led to the problem of their children's integration into British schools.

A 1971 Department of Education circular advocated a policy based on greater familiarity with immigrant communities, broader expression of cultural differences and a climate of tolerance, while remaining "concerned to protect schools from any drop in standards due to the presence of very many non-English-speaking children who might have a negative effect on the progress of the others" (quoted by Tomlinson, 1983).

This policy was translated into urban renewal programmes that developed positive discrimination measures for the benefit of badly run-down areas in the 1970s. In school curricula, both pupil textbooks and training courses for would-be teachers referred to minority cultures. Teaching of the corresponding foreign languages at school was encouraged and co-operation was sought with the representatives of minority groups (Lynch, 1983; Arora and Duncan, 1986).

The work of the Committee of Enquiry into the Education of Children from Ethnic Minority Groups resulted in two reports, one under the chairmanship of Lord Rampton (1981), and the other, Lord Swann (1985). These reports reflected the debate between:

- those (in the minority) who wished to promote equality of treatment for each individual culture. This approach could only really work with the emergence of separate schools whose intake was determined by ethnic or religious criteria, such as the Islamic schools established in the Netherlands;
- those (the majority) who called for a new universalism based on dialogue and mutual exchange (Partington, 1985).

Irrespective of the indicators adopted, most studies undertaken in the 1960s and 1970s found that children of immigrants encountered greater difficulty than British pupils. According to several such surveys, children of West Indian origin apparently performed less satisfactorily than those from other minorities. By contrast, children of Asian origin (Indians, Pakistanis and East African Asians) appeared to achieve better results. Other studies have taken a more complex view of the problem, demonstrating that differences are dependent on social background or gender, a finding corroborated by research in France and the USA. It would also seem that pupils from minority groups who possess high self-esteem do better at school but have greater difficulty in integrating within their own racial group, as well as the dominant one. On the other hand, pupils with low self-esteem are more likely to experience school failure, and to seek refuge in their home cultures from a society which they feel is hostile towards them (Taylor, 1981).

The research carried out has revealed that children from West Indian minorities are placed in proportionally greater numbers in units for mentally deficient children, counselling centres set up specially for children with behavioural problems. In the United Kingdom, there seems to be a correlation between this kind of policy, and teachers who have a stereotyped and poorly informed view of pupils from these minorities. Such an analysis points clearly to the importance of teacher training.

The survey conducted by Brittan (1976) comes to the same conclusions as those of Farkas in the USA and Payet in France. It showed that teachers had negative perceptions of West Indian background pupils. And, on the basis of a study of two comprehensive schools, Wright (1987) claims that these pupils, whether boys or girls, have been subjected to more frequent criticism, reprimand and punishment by teachers.

Needed research

In the 1990s, many researchers have criticized the naive, superficial and simplistic nature of multiculturalism which is concerned with cultural diversification, but which is either insensitive to racism, or attributes it exclusively to factors such as ignorance or teacher prejudice. As to the anti-racist perspective, it is concerned with inequalities between Blacks, Whites or Asians, as well as the various forms of domination and discrimination. Often, these studies consider that not only the curricula but the very organization of the education system needs to be changed (Troyna, 1987; Gillborn, 1996).

Research has also started to respond to the scant reference to ethnic considerations in major sociology of education and the teaching profession textbooks, and to the impact of this disregard on teacher training and the overall image of the profession (Troyna, 1994). It is thus vital that research concerned with teachers' professional identity should address questions concerned with the significance of values, the use of language at school between peers and in the classroom, and professional ethics. By doing so, it would help clarify how teachers relate to ethnic issues, while also incorporating the theme of racism (Payet, 1996).

How heterogeneous are pupils?

Teaching in schools where the majority of pupils are from disadvantaged milieux and confronted with major social and economic problems paradoxically results in a focus on two equally critical difficulties: the simultaneous management of the homogeneity and heterogeneity of pupils. Homogeneity may be regarded as a feature of the living and housing conditions of pupils whose families are hit by crisis, unemployment and exclusion. Heterogeneity, on the other hand, is evident in the following:

- widely differing levels of school performance;
- particular kinds of personal relations and know-how;
- culturally and linguistically diverse lifestyle;
- different religions.

The number of foreign pupils in a school is indeed a key factor. In some institutions, over 80 per cent of the pupils come from cultures or nationalities different from those of the host country. This kind of situation gives rise to parallel lack of understanding on the part of both pupils and schoolteachers:

- failure of the pupils to relate to either the cultural, social, and philosophical norms or the values of the school;
- incomprehension on the part of teachers regarding the behaviour of pupils. Teachers need to be responsible for encouraging effective learning strategies beyond their traditional knowledge transmission roles, even if some pupils acquire these strategies within the family.

Heterogeneity is also characteristic of the increasing number of adolescents who, outside school hours, work in big supermarkets, service stations or markets. How can one motivate pupils living as couples, sometimes with no permanent address and totally separated from their families, to continue their schooling, especially in vocational secondary schools?

Recognizing diversity and richness of different cultural groups by integrating them in a shared educational strategy

Promoting essential values

The preparation of future teachers in handling these problems involves promoting essential values, in pre-service training:

- respect for others;
- equality of opportunity, emphasizing respect for cultural diversity and fighting racism and xenophobia.

As indicated in the report of the ETUCE/CSEE (European Trade Union Committee for Education) on teacher training, "intercultural/ multicultural education must be an underlying principle within teacher education. Intercultural education and multicultural education are two of the most widely recognized terms. Whatever the terminology, we believe that the concept must be all-embracing: it must acknowledge the diversity and richness of different cultural groups, including migrants, settled ethnic minority populations, traveller communities and refugees. It must also recognize the problems of xenophobia, racism and discrimination which these groups often face, and the need for both positive approaches supporting cultural diversity and strong anti-racist policies. Education is one key area in which these social issues must be addressed" (ETUCE/CSEE, 1994).

If pre-service teacher training is to play what we regard as an essential role, training courses that take account of the diversity and richness of cultures in society will have to be developed. The capacity to foster communication and co-operation within heterogeneous ethnic groups themselves will also be one of the skills teachers need to possess.

Policies for integration and remedial education

Various structures have been developed in France to encourage scholastic achievement for young people of immigrant origin to facilitate their integration in French society. As pointed out in a Ministry of Education circular dated September 1994, "in France, national and republican ambitions have merged within a special concept of citizenship. By its nature, this French idea of the Nation and the Republic is respectful of all convictions, especially those that are religious and political, as well as cultural traditions. But it rules out the fragmentation of the Nation into mutually indifferent separate communities that are mindful only of their own rules and laws and the need to coexist. The nation is not only a body of citizens possessing individual rights. It is a community with a common destiny...." (Ministry of Education circular on confessional or similar items worn conspicuously in school, 20 September 1994).

According to the French view of integration, school thus has a twofold purpose:

- to ensure that all pupils do well, regardless of their social, cultural or geographical origin;
- to develop a sense of belonging to the same community of future citizens.

Within this framework, various measures have been introduced to facilitate the schooling of foreign pupils. For those aged from seven to ten, orientation and remedial teaching may be provided in so-called classes d'initiation (CLIN) and *cours de rattrapage intégré* (CRI) respectively. The CLIN offer tuition suited to relatively small groups of pupils (15 maximum). Their purpose is to integrate pupils as rapidly as possible within the classes corresponding to their age. The CRI are attended by pupils in ordinary classes who receive seven to eight hours' intensive tuition in French. For pupils older than 10, there are reception and integration classes, known as *classes d'accueil*. Depending on the school, their operation may differ to include:

- special classes with more French in the timetable;
- tuition in 'French as a foreign language', in special groups, while remaining in regular classes for the rest of the school day.

To meet the needs of teaching staff, 23 information and training centres for the primary schooling of children of migrants (CEFISEM, or Centres de formation et d'information pour la scolarisation des enfants de migrants) have been set up since 1975. Their purpose is to help schools, in ways that suit them, to retrain teachers or develop new teaching methods. Teachers may thus benefit from measures in areas such as the following:

- information;
- pre-service and in-service training;
- help and advice for educational teams;
- research;
- development of informational and methodological tools.

The CEFISEM in France are especially active in the ZEPs since, as a 1992 report showed, "the proportion of foreign pupils is one of the most distinguishing features of ZEP schools, as compared with those elsewhere; there are 2.7 times more foreign pupils in ZEP primary institutions, and 2.3 times more in lower-secondary ones in these areas" (Auduc, 1994).

Intercultural education

In **Switzerland**, teachers work in classes that are increasingly heterogeneous. In Geneva, 41 per cent of primary-school children are foreigners. As a result, teacher training content is increasingly concerned with family/school relationships, and intercultural matters, etc.

Confronted with the heterogeneity of pupils in **Germany**, the *Länder* have developed activities to make schools more open towards their neighbourhoods, encouraging bilingualism where the proportion of foreign pupils is very high. Thus in several schools with a large Turkish community intake, Turkish-speaking teachers have been employed to support their regular teaching colleagues, and encourage a process of integration in the host country, which builds on a gradually developed dialogue rather than a split between cultures. The *Länder* have also introduced various measures to provide specific training for teachers who will work with children or young people from a foreign background at primary and secondary levels. They include compulsory training for those studying for a teacher's diploma, additional coursework leading to the acquisition of further qualifications, in-service training, and further training. These various courses cover the following aspects:

- an introduction to educational problems associated with the integration of foreigners into German society, and a presentation of the situation in the countries of origin;
- an introduction to methods of teaching German as a second language, as well as methods for teaching other subjects in the same second language;
- teaching of core subjects in the native languages of the main groups of foreign pupils at school in Germany.

In **Denmark**, it has been decided not to create special classes for migrant children, but to provide intensive courses in Danish given by specially trained Danish teachers. The latter take a supplementary course at the Royal Danish School.

In **Italy**, immigration is a recent problem. In 1990, a circular from the Ministry responsible for education emphasized that "intercultural education must be universally introduced in all disciplines, even where there are no foreign pupils, in order to prevent the development of stereotypes and ethnocentrism".

The issue of mother-tongue education

Policies for the teaching of native languages and cultures vary strongly with country. The English-speaking countries prefer teaching to be conducted in the mother tongues. By contrast, France considers its national language to be a vehicle for the values of the Republic.

Although these mother tongues are classified as 'modern languages', they pose special teaching problems. Even where they are not perfectly mastered, they are part of the daily life of young people, and not totally unfamiliar to them. Teacher training, therefore, has to provide them with a methodology, a body of content, and an approach to classroom work in mother tongues which is different from that applicable to (other) foreign languages.

In **France**, even though controversial tuition in mother tongues is provided in primary education by teachers from the same country as their pupils, in secondary education, written and oral mastery of the French language is central to the strategy for the social integration of young people. From this standpoint, language maintenance in mother tongues seems to belong far more to the private than the public domain. In parallel, there are cultural schemes for teams of teachers to develop initiatives concerned, for example, with knowledge of immigrant communities and the cultures of the countries from which they originally immigrated. Since 1989, the 'composition française' (components of the French heritage) initiative has been developed in a great many schools, with the aim of enabling all pupils in the French education system to become familiar with the foreign contribution to the French cultural heritage.

In **Germany**, in *Länder* like Berlin or North Rhine-Westphalia, the term 'mother tongues' is used to refer to teaching concerned with such languages.

In **England and Wales**, children's home languages are taught as part of co-operation between the immigrant communities and local education authorities. Such co-operation has occasionally been problematic as in the Nottingham urban area where, under the influence of religious communities, parent associations for children of Pakistani origin, wished girl pupils to be exempt from education in art, music, and biology, as well as physical education. The 'national curriculum' with its so-called 'core' and 'foundation' subjects has ensured that managing diversity does not result in unequal treatment of young people where learning is concerned and does not allow for exemption on religious or other grounds.

At Gladsaxe, in **Denmark**, an experiment for integrating children of foreign origin has been developed as part of a combined scheme involving the school and various local structures. It develops bilingualism through use of bilingual teachers. There are no special classes for the children. They participate in transitional bilingual instruction to facilitate better understanding of the Danish language and education system. Intensive Danish-language courses are then provided by specially trained Danish teachers. Regular meetings with immigrant parents organized by the bilingual teachers encourage mutual understanding between them and the school administration. "Of course, not all problems are resolved, but I should like to emphasize that we have developed the wherewithal for immigrant children to reach levels of education comparable to those of their Danish classmates" (Ahmad et al., 1993, p. 72).

In the light of the very varied attitudes in European countries regarding mother tongues and cultural diversity, it is hard to decide unequivocally the best course of action. Should such languages and cultures belong exclusively to the private rather than the public domain? Isn't there a risk of aggravating scholastic and social inequality by promoting this diversity in the classroom? In fact, it seems that an educational policy of non-assimilation might acknowledge the legitimacy of teaching these pupils home languages, and act accordingly by introducing a third type of instruction for languages that would be 'neither foreign, nor the mother tongue'. This approach could also apply in the future to regional languages. The debate on mother tongue and bilingual education took a sudden new turn in the USA in June 1998. In California, transitional bilingual education using mother tongues to facilitate attainment and better mastery of English had been strongly criticized. The system of gradual progress towards bilingualism, which was organized for the benefit of 1.4 million pupils, had not been especially effective for children from Spanish-speaking countries. The school failure rate of 8.6 per cent for Whites was 12.2 per cent for African-Americans and 46.2 per cent for Hispanics.

Some felt that by prolonging the period of exposure to two cultures, the system appeared to be preventing young immigrants from integration within American society. Instead of reinforcing the children's pride in their roots, the system based on cultural diversity was felt to be resulting in structured segregation. A bill proposing to end bilingual education – the norm in public-sector schools in California – to allow solely for teaching in English, was submitted for a referendum in the state on 2 June 1998. This proposal, which was part of a policy for linguistic assimilation facilitating communication and social integration, was adopted by 67 per cent of California's five million voters.

Yet a new concern is raised if bilingual education is prohibited in California. The 'English only' approach can weaken family relations between Hispanic-background parents and their children schooled solely in English. Continued research is needed on this subject which, moreover, has political considerations.

Action concerning certain cultural and ethnic minorities

A 1994 French report shows that "the existence of nomadic young people in ZEP or 'sensitive' institutions, who reject school and display strong absenteeism, tends further to unsettle classroom activity" (Braustein and Dasté, 1994, p. 15). While this view is no doubt justified in the case of some schools, it belies the long-standing effort on the part of the educational sector to provide schooling for traveller communities, and fight against the discriminations to which they fall victim. All action concerned with this category of persons is covered by the periodical, *Interface*, published by the Centre for

Gypsy Research at the University of Paris V, René Descartes, with support from the European Union. In its different publications, the Centre refers to efforts in Europe to provide schooling for traveller communities, of whatever gypsy stock. The periodical itself argues in favour of more substantial training for teachers who work with young people from wholly or partially itinerant families.

In **Denmark**, several schemes have been started to integrate young gypsies into social and professional life. Training has been developed for teachers to acquire a basic idea of the cultural traditions of traveller communities. Some experiments have indeed concluded that, notwithstanding the many initiatives on behalf of such children, teachers feel the latter cannot benefit in any way in the case of long absences. Teaching of a highly sensitive kind has to be developed in order to establish positive relations between families and the school system. Indeed the barrier is not merely linguistic, but a view of children's education that often runs counter to the one represented by school. If teachers wish to address the problem (as they should), they need to understand the special needs and concerns through properly adapted training.

A Danish experiment[3] has shown that one-third of gypsy children who attend school complete the time spent there without major difficulty. The remaining two thirds make their unease felt in the form of long absences and a very negative opinion of how schools function, which is shared by the entire family. Indeed, some families choose to keep their children at home without understanding why they should learn to read and write, or because they believe that school is 'stealing' their children who are becoming 'too Danish'. Working groups have been set up for the collective training of teachers, social workers and school heads so that they can act together vis-à-vis families, by explaining the purpose of school and showing them that it is not seeking to destroy their traditions.

3. This experiment is the subject of an article published in *Interface*, No. 9.

In the **Netherlands** and **Spain**, the teacher training for work with the children of gypsies and travellers has developed in the following areas:

- the preparation of books for secondary teachers to help them with the schooling of these children;
- basic training about gypsy culture and its history.

A training course for specialized staff to work as mediators between gypsy communities, and school and administrative structures, has been started as part of a strategy to reduce school absenteeism.

In the **Flemish Community of Belgium**, under the Flemish Fund for the Integration of the Disadvantaged (VFIK), teachers are trained to work with staff responsible for the implementation of schemes for sociocultural activities, and development of young people's motivation, as well as the introduction of positive school counselling.

In the **United Kingdom**, a teaching kit for the training of staff has been devised. It makes teaching material available for both pre- and in-service training.

The European Union and the Council of Europe often support programmes of this kind. In recent years, the preparation of intercultural teaching materials for the children concerned, and the introduction of teacher training centred on the use of such materials, have been included in programmes funded by the European Union in Belgium, the United Kingdom, Spain, Greece, Ireland, the Netherlands, Italy, France and Germany.

Several countries, such as Denmark, France, Spain and Germany, have developed programmes aimed at recruiting teachers from among traveller communities. In such cases, these people have the further task of providing training on relevant issues to their own colleagues, and to mediators active between the families and school institution.

III. Preparing teachers to adapt content and methods to classroom diversity

Ensuring equal educational opportunity

Recognition of pupil diversity in secondary education does not mean that what is taught at school depends solely on the demand of particular social categories. School curricula throughout a given country have also to be made broadly similar.

As a result, the debate between the relative merits of centralized and decentralized education systems has led to considerable convergence of views. In the light of this problem, former differences in the developed countries between those who thought systems should be centralized and those who believed the contrary have become blurred. From these two models, very interesting combinations and hybrid forms are emerging. Centralized systems are gradually becoming more decentralized in a process of nationwide devolution enabling local and regional diversity to be fully reflected in primary and secondary schools. Meanwhile, decentralized systems are tending to standardize their curricula, as in the United Kingdom, Germany and the Netherlands, so that change can be controlled more effectively. Compulsory national curricula (which are traditional in countries such as France) are becoming increasingly common. In 1988, the United Kingdom introduced the *National Curriculum* as part of its *New Education Reform Act*. And, since 1991, the Netherlands has had nationally fixed objectives for different school subjects at each level.

How can secondary teachers develop interest in their subjects in mixed-ability classrooms?

Future secondary-school teachers (for example at French *lycées* or *collèges*) will normally have specialized at university in one or two subjects. From their first year in the teaching profession, they will be confronted by pupils being taught a range of subjects, who in general will not necessarily share their own enthusiasm for one or more preferred disciplines.

Managing the choice of teaching content

One source of difficulty is the difference between the level of knowledge acquired at university and the level that has to be taught at school. Teachers need to master both their knowledge of content and to adapt their teaching to the age and level of understanding of secondary pupils. Both competence and the ability to adapt content are necessary. Beginning a career as a teacher implies the following:

- mastering the fundamentals of one or more subjects, so as to be able to teach them;
- securing a sound grasp of the general organization of particular fields of knowledge within and around such subjects, so that teaching content is contextualized for pupils;
- mastering the specific features of the same subjects, and their possible interrelationships with similar features of other subjects;
- encouraging pupils to construct their own corpus of knowledge and develop methods for doing so.

While content teaching *per se* may sometimes be very difficult alongside other classroom responsibilities, from keeping order in the classroom to working with individual pupils, teachers must be able to vary their methods. So one of the aims of pre-service training must be to explain to would-be teachers that this necessary adaptability should not take place at the price of diluted content.

Teachers should also be able to choose the school textbooks best suited to their individual approach. In over two-thirds of all countries, they have to accept state-approved textbooks. Private publishers are not allowed to produce classroom books freely, nor can teachers choose them. In **Iceland**, school textbook publishing is state-controlled. In **Japan**, **Canada**, 21 states of the **USA**, **Luxembourg**, most **German** *Länder* and ***Portugal***, classroom use of textbooks depends on state authorization obtainable only if they

conform to predetermined criteria. In the **United Kingdom**, the head teacher decides about books after consultation with heads of subject departments. In **France**, there is no official body responsible for approving school textbooks. Private publishers compete on the open market. The decree of 16 June 1880 on primary education, and the circular of 13 October 1881 on secondary education, require that "teaching staff themselves examine and choose books made regularly available in the open market".

Adapting teaching methods without diluting content

The goal is to adapt teaching methods without diluting knowledge content. Pupils need teaching geared to their needs, so that they can acquire individual working methods as soon as possible, and discover an appropriate balance between their interests, aptitudes and learning requirements.

This goal calls for action at two levels. At *national level*, the skills that each pupil is normally meant to acquire should be defined by level of education and subject. Curricula have to define universal benchmarks which are non-negotiable in terms of expected attainment. At *school level*, there should be greater scope for devising curricular development policies geared to their intake. For all pupils to have a real chance of assimilating aspects of a single culture, approaches have to be diversified as pupil diversity dictates, with opportunities where necessary for digression, and methods geared to specific individual needs. Thus each school and class has to adopt a style of teaching such that every pupil can acquire, by different means, the knowledge considered essential in a given subject.

Mastering language skills

In most countries, the education system hinges *de facto* on written and oral mastery of the relevant language. Besides being a means of expression and knowledge, it is also implicitly the most significant means of selection at school. As a rule, official curricula are at pains to emphasize the importance of written and oral language comprehension in pupils' education.

One of the best examples is in the Italian *Scuola média*. Its curricula specify that the fundamental aims of teaching Italian are "to use the language as a tool for gathering and expressing experience of the world and of oneself". The Spanish LOGSE[4] states that in compulsory secondary education "the pupil should be able to understand and express correctly complex oral and written texts and messages". The British National Curriculum expresses the same general principle: "At 16, pupils should be able orally to express an opinion on a complex subject (...) to demonstrate their ability to adopt a critical point of view vis-à-vis the techniques and conventions of presentations (...), and to draft a text by organizing complex material". The curricula of Denmark and Sweden have long incorporated similar aims.

The aims themselves are related to the democratization of education. The rift should be ended between pupils considered eligible to perfect their linguistic ability via a mainly literary approach, and those for whom minimum basic skills are regarded as more appropriate. The curricula referred to above seek to provide all pupils with comparable skills of expression and communication, so that they share the same basis for comprehension and exchange, and thus the ability to access aspects of culture essential for them to participate in society.

The question of subject content is also connected to equality of opportunity. In order to achieve such equality, pupils from very varied social backgrounds should be taught together in the same classes as far as possible. Reduction of comprehensive schooling may prove very dangerous for those failing to select the right subject options, and lock them in dead-end situations, making their relations with the school system that much more difficult.

The relationship of young people to learning

The relationship to learning of young people from disadvantaged areas has been the subject of studies in several developed countries in recent years. What do such pupils require in order to perform well at school?

4. A law on general regulations concerning the education system.

Knowledge cannot be communicated to young people whose future appears compromised, without paying close attention to their value systems, cultural activities and aspects of their social behaviour that might reveal something about their attitudes to learning. Aspects of their progress are ambivalent. Their violent rejection of school is in proportion to the faith they have pinned on it. It is often hard for pupils to be aware of what they are lacking. Teachers should be attentive to the degree of overall consistency in these different linkages, relations, or the intelligibility of interactions, between learning (from the knowledge angle), well-being (from the standpoint of relations and education) and know-how (skills), and suggest remedial measures if they seem required.

Imparting meaning to learning

Teachers have to enable pupils to discover that learning is, first and foremost, about intending to learn, and will thus see it as something worthwhile; that learning with an aim, a purpose, will mean looking at the future in a different way.

During their training, therefore, teachers have to think closely about their duties so as to understand what is 'learning' as opposed to 'non-learning'. And on completion of this training, they should be more or less able to grasp what those who are learning do (or do not do) to accomplish (or not) the activity and, similarly, what teachers do (or do not do) to impart (or not) knowledge.

Thinking about the transmission of knowledge

The professional identity of teachers is closely associated with a particular subject area. Yet in recent years, learning has been affected by developments such that the close correspondence between school subjects and university courses has been compromised. In many countries, for example, this applies to the physical or natural sciences in which university course content no longer has its counterpart structure in secondary education. Many trainee teachers in history or literature note that, before preparing their lessons, they have to reconsider their entire content with an eye to the demands of the class. This is not simply a readjustment of level but, in their own terms, an intrinsic exercise in learning for them carried out in most cases by using the school textbooks.

This kind of situation means thinking carefully in pre-service training about the way knowledge should be transmitted, the meaning of the learning process, how it should be presented, its different stages, appropriate attainment and progress indicators and evaluation procedures. The forms of training entailed, which should be centred on certain approaches, particularly differentiated teaching methods, already exist. Confronted with a pupil in difficulty, a teacher should be able to identify the factor inhibiting progress, and see how far these socio-cognitive perceptions need to be altered for learning to proceed effectively. Teachers' efforts to understand pupil perceptions provide an opportunity for them to redefine their own.

Helping improve young people's achievement

Learning the techniques of differentiated teaching can help teachers ensure they give all pupils a chance to construct their own learning methods, and thus be instrumental in their own education. This method aims to ensure that individual pupils progress in a way that takes account of their achievements and potential so that they benefit from the teaching provided. The method is a vital part of teacher training for schools considered difficult in which – more than elsewhere – mixed-ability pupils have to learn, and the interest of the least motivated has to be aroused.

In such heterogeneous classes, it is important to respect the order of the different stages of work, and to be in control of the class as a whole. It is through teachers placing pupils in many different working situations, widely varying their own responses, and adapting learning methods as far as possible to individual needs, that differentiated teaching is gradually established. The following examples may help to illustrate the approach:

- *Alternating and adapting, as appropriate, collective and smaller group work:* basic concepts are presented in lessons with an entire class. Small group work involving different kinds of help and individually-tailored worksheets will help some pupils to get to grips with only poorly grasped fundamentals, while others move on to further related concepts, or even carry out research activity.

* *Establishing a graded approach to learning and the use of documents:* in practical activity, some pupils will work with simple documents leading them through specific graded straightforward questions while others, whose basic aim is the same, will study the same subject using more complex material with more open-ended worksheets giving scope for greater initiative.

* *Development of work in groups:* this activity encourages a creative attitude on the part of pupils, enabling them to use and organize their knowledge better. It also helps teachers to let them practise working methods, detect weaknesses and identify problems.

Here, computerized teaching methods can play a key role. Some software packages now offer graded exercises, broken down entirely into simple elements so that pupils can tackle a single concept at a time, while others lead to more advanced work. All of them seek to develop personalized independent learning. It is clear today that new technologies are gaining a foothold in schools. Thus CD-ROMs based on concrete practical experimentation, are making it easier for pupils to learn to read. Others are proving helpful in teaching history, geography, mathematics and many other subjects.

For language teaching, a system of TV video conferences has been set up in some schools in countries such as the United Kingdom, Germany, France and the Netherlands. It provides for real time interactive image and sound communication. Pupils from several schools with multimedia facilities can follow simultaneously lessons given by a single teacher to whom they are all linked via a TV screen and computer.

Constructing appropriate strategies

If young people are to do well at school when their living conditions distance them from the culture and criteria of competition there, it is important for teacher training to include several components that emphasize the following:

- structures for effective individualized and group teaching in the classroom;
- the question of equality of opportunity and, in particular, the meaning of schooling for young people from disadvantaged groups.

As part of the 'Teachers Academy' programme, a 'hands-on' experiment has been introduced in disadvantaged neighbourhoods of the USA at the initiative of Nobel Physics Laureate, Leon Lederman. It fosters a new kind of relationship with the culture of science at primary school, through encouraging interdisciplinarity, starting with pupils' own questions and engaging in practical experiments. In this way, children can carry out an entire process of scientific investigation.

The 'Teachers Academy' experiment

Nobel Physics Laureate Leon Lederman has for five years been experimenting with aspects of a special approach to teaching in publicly maintained schools in disadvantaged areas of Chicago.

"In the past 15 years, there has been outstanding progress in the physical sciences at university level, yet nobody has transferred this body of knowledge to the grass roots" he says. Consequently, he has set up a new approach to the experimental sciences, which whets children's curiosity. He has set up a teaching programme for schools with difficult pupils. To take part in it, teachers in eligible schools have to undergo long-term training involving the families of pupils.

One of the exercises for the children is called the 'Tragedy of the Lake'. They tell the story of children who go to swim at the edge of an unfortunately polluted lake. They are instructed to use a scoop to extract from a bowl, a water sample in which each polluting substance is represented by several coloured beads (pink for petroleum, blue for fertilizer, etc.). Each time they do so, a different sample is obtained. By studying it, the children have to deduce what is responsible for causing the pollution, and prepare diagrams and graphs to support their conclusions.

> The children are, therefore, involved in mathematics, arithmetic, and diagrammatic explanation, while also carrying out a process of scientific investigation and expressing themselves orally and in writing, in interaction with the teacher and in accordance with concrete methods deliberately far removed from rote theoretical learning.

During this experiment it was noted that, as pupils progress in scientific subjects, they do so in other subjects such as reading or writing too. Through keeping a regular diary of their personal experiences, children write, analyze, draw and reconstruct situations, etc. Their social behaviour also improves. This kind of 'advanced researcher/primary schoolteacher' co-operation in the USA, has also been introduced in France, thanks to another Nobel Physics Laureate, Georges Charpak. Here, similar pilot projects are in progress in schools located in disadvantaged suburbs of Paris and Lyon.

Establishing structures to address interpersonal problems in the classroom

Many structures have been established in various countries so that pupils can address interpersonal problems in class. Without undermining the role of teachers, young people can get different kinds of help for some of the problems they encounter.

In the classroom, teachers cannot take on all social welfare responsibilities. They cannot simultaneously be youth workers, social workers, judges, police officers, nurses and conveyors of knowledge. To carry out their main task of enabling pupils to acquire the knowledge they need for their education, they have to become familiar with the essential human resources present both in their school and its local area. Each category of resources has a precise function. Depending on the country, staff able to work with teachers inside and close to a school may be monitors, counsellors, school psychologists, guidance counsellors, psychologists, principal educational advisers, etc.

Where teachers are familiar with the role and specific tasks of such staff, they will be better placed to assume their responsibilities by securing support for their own action and, by the same token, gaining recognition from all these other actors. If teachers are unable by themselves to solve pupils' problems, they can call on the appropriate staff to help them. In such cases, work is conducted in a partnership in which it has to be made clear to children that, where teachers refer them to other professionals, it is not because they no longer care about their difficulties but, on the contrary, because they wish to mobilize a broader educational team effort on their behalf.

The teaching and support staff team in schools need to understand each others' potential contribution and be able to co-operate effectively.

In Hamburg, **Germany**, multi-purpose schools have introduced a system of monitors responsible for assisting pupils aged between 10 and 12, particularly where study skills need to be developed.

In **Denmark**, a system of homeroom teachers exists in primary schools and lower-secondary schools. They deal with all educational and social problems arising in the class. A special weekly 'free class discussion session' is included in the timetable.

Austria has pupil counsellors in its secondary schools. They are recruited from among teachers to play the part of information and guidance officers, as well as 'roving trouble-shooters', who are meant to help pupils overcome personal problems, and resolve tensions at school. They collaborate closely with school psychologists and are freed from one or two hours' teaching a week. Pupils, parents, colleagues and school heads can request their assistance, and their training programme includes the following:

- learning theories;
- diagnoses and individual counselling;
- socialization, behavioural motivation;
- communication and methods of conflict resolution;
- group dynamics.

In **France**, psychologist guidance counsellors (*conseillers d'orientation psychologues*, or COPs) based at information and guidance centres (*centres d'information et d'orientation*, or CIOs) – of which there is one in each district generally including several cities or towns – help pupils to devise a personal strategy, and work with teachers during special times they may actually be consulted on the school premises. Principal education advisers (*conseillers principaux d'éducation*, or CPEs) deal with daily problems at school, acting in liaison with part-time monitors, most of whom are university students. Aside from problems linked to the arrival or departure of pupils, supervision and absenteeism, the CPEs are available to help pupils make school a place for learning and the practice of citizenship with organized clubs, reception or counselling areas and training pupil representatives for school councils. Social workers or health staff (such as nurses and school doctors), may also be active at a school or exercise a supportive role on its behalf from their main office elsewhere.

The use of auxiliary staff in *collèges* and *lycées* has become more widespread in the 1990s. Many secondary schools now employ mediators to act as intermediaries between pupils, pupils and teachers, or families and school heads. They are often young people aged between 20 and 26. This category of staff have trained for two years after the Baccalaureate and obtain a five-year state contract under which they help teachers towards a better grasp of situations and forms of behaviour. Their main responsibility is to foster dialogue, helping families to access information, become more familiar with the school and school staff, and understand the way the education system works.

The presence of these specialist staff, and awareness of their role, does not absolve teachers from their responsibility for addressing aspects of school life or guidance during lessons. But they do know that they are not obliged to find all the answers, and that they can advise pupils to talk to one or several of their more specialist colleagues. The contribution of teachers to these questions, as part of their responsibilities, is especially significant when they are designated as *Professeur principal* (principal teacher or homeroom teacher) for a class. The duties of principal teachers are to coordinate dialogue between all the teachers for a given class, while also acting as the first point of contact for families and pupils on questions of guidance. Their effectiveness is essential, particularly where the school intake is considered difficult. These duties have to be a focus of pre-service training.

Tackling the question of citizenship education

The question of citizenship education is clearly of overriding importance in teacher training, during which critical appraisal of school textbooks in general use may be envisaged so that teachers can develop an individual approach to the question, independently of existing classroom material.

The issues of citizenship education or for Human and Children's Rights are often linked to discussion on the ultimate purpose of school. Just 40 years ago, 80 per cent of young people in Europe began work at the age of 14. Today, 80 per cent are still at school at the age of 17. This longer period of schooling tends to draw out the period of adolescence, with the result that schools become responsible, in some respects, for the transition of young people into adult life. And changes that have occurred in family structures and other institutions mean that schools are increasingly taking over the entire education of children. Pupils are no longer simply present for teaching, but also 'subjects' to be brought into relation with society. Such questions are of decisive significance in schools whose intake consists primarily of disadvantaged children, for school is often the only place where these young people encounter institutions and their regulations.

In 1985, the Council of Europe recommended that 'learning about Human Rights' should be taught. A 1988 report showed that this recommendation was very widely interpreted and that "teachers were often ignorant about concepts bound up with:

- identification of prejudice, stereotypes, inequality and discrimination, particularly sexism and racism;

- non-violent resolution of conflicts and the development of a sense of responsibility vis-à-vis how one acts, or does not act" (Council for Cultural Co-operation, 1988, p. 29).

As pupils in schools, young people should know what is forbidden and what is allowed, as well as what forms of behaviour are in breach of regulations. Since they are not always aware when they start school of the bounds that cannot be overstepped, it is vital that they should get to know the rules; and that, where possible, the rules should be adopted following education into citizenship, rather than being simply imposed. As Paul Martens, at the Court of Arbitration in Brussels, has said: "what is the use of theoretical learning about democratic virtues if there is no practical empirical familiarity with them?".

In order to be fully effective in this respect, teachers have to be very well acquainted with the rules of school law, as well as the internal regulations of individual schools, which together represent the rules and aims of the education system in their country.

School failure, a relative and context-bound concept

The concept of school failure does not have the same connotations in all countries. In those that do not allow pupils to repeat a school year, non-attainment by children is associated with lack of personal development, thwarted individual progress, and premature drop-out. In countries with examination systems and selective assessment, school failure is defined in terms of repeated courses, drop-out, or leaving school without a diploma.

In **Denmark**, school failure is thought to have occurred where there is an imbalance between the attainment of a pupil, his or her natural abilities and the benefit(s) he gains from teaching. Around 10 per cent of pupils quit at the compulsory school-leaving age.

In the **United Kingdom**, the term 'school failure' is not used. In England, Wales and Northern Ireland, the notion is expressed in the concept of 'underachieving' and corresponds to the situation of pupils who do not manage to achieve their individual potential. In

Scotland, the tendency is to speak of individual learning difficulties caused by a handicap (whether mental, physical, emotional or social) or inappropriate teaching methods.

In **Greece**, school failure is associated with the levels attained by pupils with respect to the aims of the curriculum. It is measured in terms of the illiteracy rate and the drop-out rate (1.8 per cent in big cities and 8.1 per cent in the provinces during the first three years of lower secondary education, according to 1990 figures).

In **Portugal**, the concept relates primarily to the inability of pupils to achieve aims defined globally for each stage of study. The main indicators are grade repetition rates, drop-out and examination. The first stood at around 23 per cent at primary level, and 14.9 per cent at the end of lower-secondary education in 1992.

In **Italy**, school failure or *dispersione scolastica* is measured by drop-out rates and percentage of grade repetition among an age group (12.1 per cent in lower-secondary school in 1991).

In **Spain**, the law on general regulations for the education system (LOGSE) defines school failure as "special difficulty in attaining the general aims established for basic education".

In **Belgium**, school failure is defined in terms of unachieved cognitive objectives.

Each year, pupils discontinue their studies along the way, without completing the stage of the curriculum they have begun, or even sitting the corresponding examinations. Very discreetly or very abruptly, they 'give up'. Whether the expression used is 'drop-out' as in the United Kingdom, *disperzione scolastica* (Italy), or *décrocheurs scolaires* (Canada), several countries formally identify the phenomenon of school drop-out, and attempt to implement arrangements for 'a fresh start' in order to forestall it, or help pupils catch up.

Whether it is viewed in terms of faltering individual progress, grade repetition, unqualified school-leavers or drop-out, school failure always represents the failure of the education system to achieve real equality of opportunity, despite all efforts to do so. "It is also an indication of the difficulty of both trying to achieve quality education and providing an adequate level of education for all, so as to give everyone a chance to play a full part in society" (EURYDICE, 1994).

As part of the fight against school failure, several countries have developed pre-schooling for three-six-year-olds. A substantial body of research has pointed to the positive influence of such arrangements and their duration, on subsequent studies. They enable possible pupil difficulties to be detected at a very early stage and thus constitute a key element in measures to combat school failure.

IV. Managing problems of authority, discipline, absenteeism and aggressive behaviour

Are schools areas of unrest?

Whereas in the past, young people often began their working life in adolescence, young people today remain in the school system for a long time. If a school is a place of daily democratic conduct, the micro-society that it represents will no doubt achieve its own integrity, forms of arbitration and working rules. Given the violence that exists around it, how can such a community develop a collective reflex for self-defence?

This question is of considerable relevance for, in a great many countries, the focus of public debate on urban security has gradually shifted from the street towards the school. Schools are now identified as areas of possible unrest in their own right, in the same way as sports grounds, public transport in cities or neighbourhoods.

What is described as undisciplined behaviour

Various surveys in France (Ministry of Education, Direction de l'Evaluation et de la Prospective, 1992-94) have shown that among *lycée* or *collège* teachers, 46.5 per cent of women and 31.5 per cent of men have very often or quite often had to deal with undisciplined pupil behaviour. Figures stand at 58.5 per cent for teachers aged less than 25, 70.5 per cent for those in ZEP institutions (and 76 per cent for those who have just begun teaching). By type of institution, 58 per cent have had discipline-related problems in *collèges*, compared to 34 per cent in vocational *lycées* and 27 per cent in *lycées*. More teachers of language, history, philosophy and such subjects, mainly women, confront lack of discipline at school, than those in technological subjects, mainly men, who seem to experience relative calm.

When first-time teachers are asked about the reasons for such problems, they refer to the following: pupils who tend to cause trouble (60 per cent), oversize classes (39 per cent), social problems of some pupils (33 per cent), lack of interest in the subject among pupils (25 per cent) or mixed-ability classes (24 per cent).

When confronted with undisciplined behaviour patterns that make demands on both the social responsibilities of teachers and their teaching skills, first-time teachers attempt primarily to establish or re-establish a dialogue with the pupils concerned. When one or more pupils upset classroom activity, teachers consider that the most appropriate responses are to reason with them (70 per cent), give them some work (41 per cent), or temporarily stop the class (31 per cent).

Yet lack of discipline is not necessarily synonymous with aggressive behaviour. There is a difference between disturbance caused by one pupil in the class and acts of violence, which needs to be addressed in pre-service training to avoid confusion. The focus has to be on the attitude of teachers vis-à-vis aspects of undisciplined conduct, so that they can be helped to consolidate their authority. The problems responsible for acts of violence at school have to be dealt with separately, while bearing in mind that failure to control classroom disturbances may result in aggressive forms of behaviour.

However, it is inappropriate for pre-service training to lend credence to teachers' preconceptions by describing any undisciplined act as 'violence'. Yet it is important to bear in mind that, in some 'difficult' schools, violence is just below the surface and apparent in the violent language. These forms of expression seem 'natural' to pupils who cannot understand why adults are disturbed. Fairly obviously, the language used by pupils and that of teachers is dissimilar. They do not speak the same language either formally, or psychologically. Furthermore, while pupils usually talk unrestrainedly, what they write often leaves much to be desired [5].

5. See chapter III, p.63, *Mastering language skills.*

Addressing violence at school

It would seem, therefore, that pre-service training for those intending to teach should define the reference frameworks and conceptions that have led all those internally involved in schools – pupils, teachers, heads, and representatives of the governing authorities – as well as external actors too – the police, judicial authorities, social workers and locally elected representatives – to determine their policy and attitudes vis-à-vis violence. Violence at school has to be clearly understood during pre-service training, given the considerable anxiety it causes future teachers.

It is no doubt worth recalling that violence has always existed in collective and sometimes spectacular forms, as well as in personal relationships between individuals. Neither has it always created a sense of insecurity. As a rule, it previously assumed ritualized forms, affecting only a limited proportion of young people. It also reinforced the power of the law – both the school and its agents – by providing a means for it to display its supremacy.

But its implications are very different today now that violence at school is such a serious subject of social concern. Extensively highlighted by the media, this violence is giving rise to considerable anxiety, for it is viewed as the tip of the iceberg, and a sign that schools are unable to carry out their responsibility of preparing young people for life in society. Up against the challenge of the severest forms of misconduct, as well as the most commonplace, such as those subsumed under the heading of insolence, schools demonstrate their total inability to keep order, so that society is left feeling utterly helpless.

No doubt when schools experience a challenge to their legitimacy with their guiding principles compromised, circumstances are conducive to the emergence of deviant behaviour and violence. Either are a consequence and sign of unrest deriving from factors external to a school (such as unemployment) and the inability of the institution to preserve its credibility as a social agency responsible for integration.

Forms of violence

The different forms of violence have been classified. According to J. Hebert (1991), its various forms are as follows:

- physical violence, bodily violence, aggressive acts and self-mutilation;
- material forms of violence;
- oral violence, insults, threats or humiliation;
- symbolic and/or ritual forms: ragging, stigmatization or creation of scapegoats.

They trigger off numerous patterns of social reaction:

- the logic of authority and redefinition of the relation between what is legal and what is legitimate;
- the logic of institutionalization;
- economic logic, or that of the parallel economy where there is drug-dealing or racketeering;
- the logic of urbanization;
- symbolic logic;
- the logic of initiation rites.

Arguably three major kinds of violence can be more clearly defined:

1. Verbal, physical or juvenile violence, nearly always related to regulations and forms of sociability restricted to a particular age group. Some writers in France and North America have pointed out that in the former working-class world, juvenile violence was not merely recognized, but almost legitimized and part of a body of structured social relations (Chesnais, 1981).

2. Anti-school forms of violence, challenging a particular teaching relationship or normative model particular to school.

3. Social forms of violence that infiltrate schools because of openness to external social phenomena (rackets, drugs, sexual assault, etc.).

While verbal violence is the foremost anxiety among teachers, it is up to a point commonplace within schools. 'It's the way we always speak' say young people themselves when pulled up for uncouth language. When pupils behave in a way that is borderline, staff are confronted with adolescents for whom the rules of society lack meaning, as everyday forms of communication are not considered important. In this way, violence may become their only mode of expression. Aggressiveness among pupils is intensifying while, vis-à-vis adults, it is also increasingly self-evident. To some extent, violence against teachers is perceived by all pupils including those who are failing as unacceptable. However, this is not always true of violence directed at unskilled and service staff who are often its first victims. This is why the unwavering solidarity of all adults in a school when faced with serious breaches of conduct by pupils is so important.

If staff have not been prepared for these situations in their pre-service training, they may feel that pupils are living 'on another planet' and that 'school knowledge is, for them, a form of assault'. Nevertheless, the school norm is clearly one that pupils continue to internalize in some form.

Factors in violence

During their training, future teachers should be told without hesitation that stability in schools may be very delicately poised, and constantly under threat. No problems can be regarded as permanently solved, and an incident within or outside the school can be enough to lead to renewed disorder. It is therefore important for teachers to be aware of the permanent need to maintain respect for school rules.

Surveys conducted in most industrialized countries point to a slow but unmistakable shift in violence into school classrooms. In penetrating the class itself, violence is liable to be perceived more sharply, by becoming more visible and setting itself more firmly against the specific purpose of school. Thus a small marginal group of very hard and repeatedly absent pupils is now observable, and gradually increasing in size from year to year. In France, this core is thought to represent 5 per cent of pupils, the same proportion noted in so-called 'sensitive' areas.

What sort of consideration should be given in training to the factors that trigger violence at school? The first step is to identify the different factors possible.

1. The violence directed against teachers by pupils does not appear to be uniform. On occasions, it reflects pupil resentment towards teachers viewed as too disdainful or, conversely, opposition towards young teachers who have been unable to command respect. It may also be the sign of a sexist attitude towards women teachers, or hostility to teachers who maintain a superior and distant attitude from their pupils. While raising these various points is interesting, it is neither a formal enumeration, nor training in itself. Nevertheless, it provides a basis for identifying attitudes that are best avoided, such as scorn, aloofness, provocation, over-familiarity and so forth.

2. The school may generate factors which can trigger off violence: poorly maintained premises, inappropriate teaching methods, the absence of internal regulations, poorly organized courses and timetables, failure of teachers to listen to pupils, etc. Teachers must be able to detect these weaknesses and seek to remedy them, with support from the entire teaching staff.

3. Violence at school is fuelled by violence from outside it. It may be linked to family violence, 'abdication' on the part of parents, absenteeism, and poorly maintained law and order within neighbourhoods, etc. In general, organized gang warfare occurs outside schools. Violence of this kind, sometimes with racist overtones, meets with ongoing retaliatory violence in exceptionally tough areas where authority has completely broken down outside the school.

The logical sequence that follows is obvious, as violence leads to theft, racketeering and the refusal to speak out against offenders through fear or complicity in a trend already afflicting a significant number of schools.

Schools are not a mirror image of circumstances outside them

Analysis of this situation outside the school has to be a part of training, so that future teachers can understand how too many young people reach school keenly traumatized by circumstances such as unemployed parents, exclusion, and fragmented families. Yet it should not be overlooked that, while school is a mirror of social life, albeit slightly distorted, it is not an entirely faithful mirror because it reflects and presents the local environment around it in its own way. Although school cannot be expected to solve all problems, it must at least be given the means to fulfil its responsibilities.

Pre-service training has to emphasize that school is responsible for young people at an age where they have reached a critical turning point. It is the age at which they are in search of their identity vis-à-vis themselves and others, the age at which one needs sound bearings, if not full-blown social and school initiation rituals. Yet young people gnawed by the crisis are suffering from a lack or total loss of such indicators. School is often the only place at which there are operational rules and a reference system for young people at odds with an environment frequently dominated by survival of the fittest. It is thus desirable that the way the institution operates should help to exert a positive influence on what occurs in its vicinity.

Naturally, the school's officials have no power to intervene directly in what goes on outside it, even if this can give rise to deviant behaviour on its premises. Yet action within schools to prevent absenteeism and apathy at school, to develop young people's sense of responsibility and give expression to solidarity and fellowship, may help to promote positive values, and influence conduct in the neighbourhood of the school. As a result, school may have a truly effective role as a place for knowledge and the emergence of citizenship.

Reducing the aggressiveness of pupils

In order to determine how aggressiveness is to be limited, it is essential to decode what is said. In their acts of violence, young people often express real problems, and those who are on the receiving end are not necessarily those for whom the violence was intended. Faced with aggressive behaviour by young people, teachers have to learn how to react:

- by applying the law and regulations, limits not to be overstepped;
- by not giving way to feelings of guilt, or constantly questioning their own judgement.

The adult must accept the role of representative of the law, that of the person who fixes the limit not to be transgressed. A conciliatory form of sanction that distinguishes between the act and the person who committed it has to be established. This, again, implies a different approach to teaching, and the drawing up of a contract between teachers and taught, whose tenor is constantly renegotiated. It is thus essential that training should provide time for consideration of matters relating to school life, and the conflict settlement, but also examination of methods out in the community with staff from the police, the judicial authorities and neighbourhood youth workers to establish closer links so that certain conflicts can be tackled more effectively.

Regardless of whether the persons involved are teachers, assistant social workers, youth workers, representatives of the police or judicial authorities, all those whose task it is to teach, take preventive action, support or punish, need to work together on questions relating to violence, while fully respecting each other's skills and the complementary roles required of them. They must do so also in the conviction that, while intervention should be timely, it should not degenerate into precipitate haste.

Moreover, all educational methods are not on the same footing as regards cognitive development:

- Educational methods rooted in extreme authoritarianism are not conducive to clear identification of the cognitive and social rules, together with their conventions, that are the means to intellectual autonomy.

- Laxness deprives children of the stable reference system that is vital for mobilizing cognitive ability and the development of reasoning.

A flexible form of education that encourages the awareness of rules and the development of autonomous strategies, results in improved use of cognitive and relational capacity.

National initiatives

A survey in the Netherlands

In 1992-93, the Ministry of Education in the **Netherlands** commissioned a survey at the Institute of Applied Social Sciences of the University of Nijmegen, on violence in secondary schools. Among the pupils, 15 per cent admitted they had been victims of physical violence on at least one occasion, while 43 per cent said they had suffered damage to belongings or other forms of mistreatment. The study has revealed that violence in schools tends to be conditioned more by outside factors.

"Settled, ordered classes at school result from clear precise identification of disciplinary rules and constant attention focused on the problems of pupils (...). Establishing a positive social bond between pupils and their school is an important means of forestalling violence. Such social bonding can be reinforced through the creation of small groups in which pupils work together, in giving them a greater sense of responsibility, and in getting them to work in accordance with their own level and in their own way" (Secretary of State for Education, 1994).

On the basis of these results, the Ministry of Education decided to launch, in 1995, a three- or four-year programme against violence at school. It includes the following:

- the introduction of mediators selected from among the teaching or administrative staff, or even the pupils themselves, who have to deal with all conflicts arising between pupils, and between teachers and pupils;

- the establishment of special areas in which pupils can meet, and organize and carry out activities together.
- the granting of new responsibilities to young people in managing school resources and in selection of subjects for their courses.

As a result of these provisions, the incidence of acts of violence in schools appears to have levelled out, although such acts persist, in particular because of the increase in inter-ethnic conflicts in the big cities.

Initiatives common to several countries

Initiatives common to teacher trade unions in the regions of Lorraine in **France, Luxembourg** and the Sarre *Land* in **Germany** were formulated in October 1994 on the theme 'Keep Violence out of School' and led to recommendations for 'provisions to counter acts of violence committed by young people'.

Working groups common to the three countries were organized on themes such as the media and violence, racism and violence, unemployment, family circumstances and violence and school structures and violence. Among the recommendations of these groups were the following:

- the setting up of school-based schemes to give greater responsibility and autonomy to young people, and familiarize them with the cultural diversity in their midst;
- to use information and communication technologies to bring schools in the three countries into contact with each other, and with schools in developing countries;
- to draft internal school rules regulations together with pupils.
- to implement initiatives with local authorities and firms, which are intended to help pupils secure a job as rapidly as possible when they leave school;
- to organize regular meetings with school heads, teachers, pupils, journalists and media representatives to avoid sensationalizing

conflicts that erupt in schools or their neighbourhoods, and to reduce excessive violence in the audiovisual media in general.

Mediation in the USA

The **USA** is in an unusual position because of the presence of gangs as yet unknown in other countries. Before entering school premises, pupils are frisked or electronically searched to detect the possible presence of weapons. The response to this situation has been to develop mediation schemes (some 2,000 schemes are currently under way), based on the principle that schools suffer from a control deficit because traditional forms of authority are not adapted to the settlement of this kind of conflict.

This *mediation* is a new method of controlling conflict, and makes use of communication and negotiation techniques. Its aim is not simply to respond to immediate problems facing schools, such as violence, vandalism and absenteeism. It also incorporates a teaching aspect in the form of a new method for settling disputes.

A programme developed in the Middle Country School District of New York State provides for the training of teachers and/or pupils to mediate in conflicts among pupils, or between pupils and parents. It is a *mixed kind of mediation* insofar as it brings together, as mediators, teachers and pupils, but *restricted* in that the latter only handle conflicts among pupils or between pupils and parents. Disputes between teachers and pupils are not subject to mediation.

The Conflict Managers Project initiated by the Community Board of San Francisco seeks to implement meditation by peers, which is conducted by pupils during conflicts among themselves. Adults are not involved in these procedures that take place during recess.

A first assessment shows that 134 cases were submitted to mediators during a single year. Out of these cases, 116 actually led to mediation, with an agreement reached in 96 instances. The number of children kept away from school for brawling dropped by half in the schools concerned.

On the basis of this work and in liaison with the National Association for Mediation in Education (NAMES), the New Mexico Center for Dispute Resolution of Albuquerque and the School Mediation Associates Center of Boston, France is now attempting to experiment with similar arrangements (in schools attached to the *Académies* – the local education authorities – of Rouen and Lyon). The aim is to heighten the interest of pupils in the following:

- use of non-violent means for settling petty daily conflicts (arguments, insults, borrowing belongings, etc.);
- the need for listening on both sides, for communication in an attempt to try and understand the attitudes and reasons that motivate the conflicting parties;
- learning methods of reasoning in order to seek solutions to conflicts (apologies, making amends);
- the importance of their own responsibilities (NAMES, 1989).

Naturally, these initiatives go hand in hand with action aimed at heightening parallel interest – on the part of the whole educational community and the parents of pupils – in conflict management via mediation. Training has been developed for pupils, with a view to the mediation of conflict among them, and for teachers and parents, for the mediation of conflict between them too. The course focuses on conflict analysis, listening and mediation techniques.

Preventive action in the United Kingdom

In the **United Kingdom**, the Ministry of Education has in recent years proposed a series of measures inspired by a preventive approach, to reduce disruptive behaviour in schools. The approach entails daily monitoring of pupil behaviour inside school, for which teachers and heads get special preparation. It also challenges the assumption that disruptive acts should go unreported through fear or complicity. In a 1987 report on violence in the United Kingdom, systematic reporting of acts of violence appeared to have a preventive impact.

As part of their training, teachers are made aware not only of the need to report violent conduct and ensure that bullying or assault are punished, but of the benefits of highlighting non-violent forms of behaviour. The committee for the preparation of school curricula has published a handbook entitled *Finding answers to disruption: discussion exercises for secondary teachers.* This guides teachers through a structured process for evaluating and changing their teaching methods, which encourages small-group pupil activity to develop young people's autonomy and teamwork. It is also intended that secondary-school teachers should co-ordinate their activities more with teachers of other subjects, so that real teaching teams are developed.

All schools practise methods of tutoring, for which future teachers are prepared. Two days are devoted to this in their training lasting a year. Furthermore, two-thirds of their time in pre-service training has to be spent within schools where they assume responsibility for tutoring a group of pupils.

Co-operation between institutions in France

For the purpose of handling aggressive behaviour in **France**, experimental partnerships have been developed between state education and the police and judicial authorities. This co-operation makes for joint inter-professional deliberation on these matters which, while considering the issue of the law with its codes and ritual, also highlights the crucial role of other social institutions and the children's environment.

It is at this focal point of the various approaches that responses to the basic difficulties of young people who actually transgress are to be found. They involve a view of the law as a mechanism for organizing relations between human beings. As part of the 'Policy for the City', local facilities have been set up by the police and judicial bodies. Because they are intended to deliver a faster more lightweight reaction to relatively minor acts of delinquency, these arrangements alter the relations between schools, the courts and the police. They provide for intervention on the part of the institutions normally concerned, without resulting in formal charges and legal proceedings.

Arrangements of this kind have to be described in pre-service training so that teachers understand the range, monitoring procedures and complementary nature of these initiatives, with reference to concrete examples, such as the following:

- area police officers whose presence alone near the entrance to schools can help to preserve calm and maintain order without any repressive action;

- police staff who respond to certain offences with an admonition, a firm but non-offensive talking-to, or escort back to school premises any adolescent truants they may encounter;

- magistrates who take action in juvenile 'houses of justice' and, by means of mediation or compensation, or warnings with reference to the law, manage to resolve conflicts linked to some penal offences, out of court;

- some services for the legal protection of young people, which assist school disciplinary councils.

As a result of their training, teachers should realize that the increased presence of the police and judiciary in or near schools should not lead them to tune their teaching methods to action by either of these two institutions, but allow them to offload some problems associated with delinquency that they are unable to handle themselves.

Partnership also extends to other institutions, such as the public transport authorities. In 'difficult' neighbourhoods, often the only two institutions present are schools and bus companies which are also the victims of vandalism and violence, etc. Forms of co-operation include the following:

- bus-drivers giving talks in schools;
- bus-drivers working jointly with teachers;
- visits to bus depots;
- joint production of teaching materials, involving bus companies and state education.

In the Paris region, a day of training on these topics is organized jointly by the *Régie autonome des transports parisiens* (RATP), the nationalized transport company for metro and bus services in the Paris area, and the Ministry of Education.

The Fight against violence at school in Seine-Saint-Denis
(the eastern suburbs of Paris)

In 1992, a joint note was drawn up by the *Académie* inspectorate and the main court public prosecutor. Its aim was to facilitate implementation of a privileged partnership between, on the one hand, school heads and the *Académie* inspectorate and, on the other, the public prosecutor for juvenile offences and the police.

In its second paragraph, this note states: "For a long time, forms of violence that appear in school communities have been of concern to school heads and, more broadly, all bodies and professions involved in problems of justice and of an educational nature. It seems essential that, in incidents that clearly have a legal aspect, school heads should be able to benefit from police and judicial support".

The same note also makes it possible for heads to deal with problems when penal offences are committed within schools, or in cases of educational assistance or where a young person is not attending school, by offering them immediate access to a specialized full-time magistrate from the prosecutor's department, who can advise them as to the appropriateness of the proposed course of action and take the necessary steps to monitor its outcome.

The note further provides for the *Académie* inspectorate and school heads to be kept informed of judicial decisions, and for an account of measures introduced by educators, with judicial authorization, to be circulated so as to foster relations beneficial to educational activity with teachers.

According to the first deputy court public prosecutor at Bobigny "the impact of this note was substantial and immediate. It led to action for the prompt resolution of most punishable or criminal offences committed in schools. In so doing, it also ended any impression on the part of young people that such offences go unpunished, encouraged pupils to report them, contrary to their conventional reticence, and also greatly diminished the sense of insecurity often experienced by teaching staff, along with the feeling that very little was done to support them (...) State education now appears to be behind only the police and social services in reporting disturbing incidents or offences.

In the first three months of 1994, schools reported 153 cases to the public prosecutor for juvenile offences, as follows :

- 85 related to offences that included 21 instances of insulting and threatening behaviour, and 37 cases of assault, five of them by gangs, and eight involving weapons;
- 62 concerned increasingly disturbing conduct on the part of young people;
- 6 related to absenteeism from school.

In June 1994, progress on these cases was as follows:

- *for the 85 offences,* 21 had gone to court, 26 resulted in no further action subject to educational monitoring procedures, 23 led to investigation proceedings, and 15 to 'police warnings'
- *in the case of the 62 'formally identified pupils',* 30 were 'already known', 17 were being monitored by the service for judicial protection of young people in receipt of educational support, 14 were subject to investigation; proceedings, and one case had been filed after investigation
- *as regards the 6 cases of 'absenteeism from school',* 3 were 'already known', and 3 were being monitored by the service for judicial protection of young people in receipt of educational support.

Prepared on the basis of documents made available by the Inspectorate of the Académie of Seine-Saint-Denis and the Bobigny court public prosecutor, as well as the article by Pierre Moreau, First Deputy Court Public Prosecutor at Bobigny (Historiens-Géographes, *1995 n° 346*).

Providing a reference system for young people

The social effectiveness of schools is judged in terms of their capacity to establish systems of reference indicators and rules, as well as to impart knowledge. Yet they also have to define their perspective clearly in the training they offer their staff. While schools are among several public and private facilities that regularly inhabit the daily life and physical surroundings of workaday areas or extensive modern blocks of flats, they are the sole common facility in any neighbourhood to bring as many people together all at once. This observation applies as much to schools in modern urban residential areas as those elsewhere. Care should be taken not to immediately equate vast blocks of flats in a city with systematically difficult circumstances. In Liverpool, the neighbourhoods considered to be most in difficulty comprise small red brick houses while, in Prague, the residents in big blocks of flats are better off than average, since their accommodation is more comfortable than older Czech houses.

The school class is the basic unit, the protected and privileged area. It is the class, rather than the school itself, which may be regarded as a sanctuary. Ideally, both the class and school institution would be simultaneously removed from the world yet fully 'plugged into its daily life'. It is for this reason that school should play a part in constructing a reliable system of reference indicators, which are vital for a young person in a society where they are not always self-evident:

- spatial indicators: a sense of scale, architecture and the environment;
- temporal indicators: organization of daily activity, lessons, tutorials, sports;
- indicators associated with authority: knowledge of regulations, law and rights;
- indicators related to subject knowledge;
- indicators as regards places for talking and listening;
- indicators vis-à-vis the adult world, which implies considering a real community of administrative and service staff, workers and teaching staff bound together by a common purpose.

The establishment of a system of reference indicators is also about developing the young people's autonomy, by which is meant the right to establish their own rules. Before they can do so, they must understand the purpose of such rules and why they are useful. Learning to live in a community implies not only fundamental acceptance of certain laws beyond dispute, but contributing with others to shape rules required for coexistence. Young people are especially motivated when they are the creators of such rules. To make them autonomous beings is to provide them with access to the three acts that regulate collective existence:

(i)   fixing the rules;
(ii)   seeing that they are applied;
(iii) administering justice.

At the same time, they are initiated into dialogue and discussion. Time, trial and error, experimentation and mistakes are all required before rules are fully consolidated. This period of experimentation by young people has to be managed patiently.

On the basis of this kind of learning, young people acquire autonomy because they can relate to values (allowing the weakest to express themselves, respecting the freedom of one's neighbour, helping others) and because they have grasped the necessity for law. Of course, this work with rules (and it has to be repeated during training that there is no panacea) does not prevent all conflicts, but it may assist the development of a capacity to resolve conflicts positively, with self-confidence and the ability and willingness to listen and communicate.

The work entailed is particularly important in that all surveys of school populations considered difficult reveal that one of the main characteristics of the pupils concerned is inability to follow the rules of school and life in society.

Pupil participation

The ways in which pupils take part in school administration and activity differ according to country.

In Greece, participation is devised through student communities, the *Mathitikes Kinotites*, both in each class and the school as a whole. Strongly organized in secondary education, these pupil councils are active in the areas of school and disciplinary problems.

In Denmark, all pupils not only have the right, but are also obliged to participate in decisions taken in collaboration with teachers on the content, forms and methods of teaching. Pupil councils are compulsory in all schools, provided pupils wish them to be established, and represent the interests of children vis-à-vis municipal and regional educational authorities.

In Germany, pupil participation is organized from primary level by means of the election of class delegates. From secondary education onwards, all kinds of schools provide for pupil representation at both institutional and *Länd* level.

The responsibilities of these bodies include, in particular, participation in educational activity, defending the collective interest of pupils and participation in the school council. Pupils are represented at secondary school level in Belgium (participatory council), France (the school board), in Italy, Spain (school council), and in Portugal.

Responding to pupils' need to be heard

Schools and their staff must be familiar with problems that exist in their local environment and, in particular, several questions concerning 'deviant behaviour' by young people.

Drug abuse is not merely experienced in terms of dealing in drugs, but also by pupil consumers who fast become victims rather than delinquents. Drug-taking and gradual alcoholism often represent an escape from the suffering experienced by pupils. This is the suffering of children who may have been battered, undernourished, rejected by their parents, faced with very serious family situations, and totally overcome by problems far more telling and intractable than lessons in mathematics or science. But 'cries for help' may assume other forms, including anorexia, suicide attempts, taking of tranquillizers or premature motherhood, all of which should be taken very seriously.

Schools have to be capable of registering these many different kinds of pressure. Often, pupils most vulnerable to the risk of AIDS are the least well informed about the various precautions against it. Teachers need to know how to identify pupils who are hoping for consideration and attention, or are very deeply depressed, so that they can direct them towards skilled support from educational staff, or the nursing or social welfare sectors.

A secondary school, such as a *collège* or *lycée*, seems to offer an environment for consolidating firm social roots and a reference system, for which it would be hard to find a suitable replacement. Indeed, for young people with problems, above all, "it may be the only environment in which they feel looked after (notwithstanding attendant restrictions), listened to and cared for, and to which they can return looking foolish, denying the obvious and without bravado, after getting into trouble of one sort or another" (Braunstein and Dasté, 1994, p. 32).

Pupils considered difficult need to be 'respected'. This almost obsessive search for respect may be reflected in commonplace violence. The twofold need for affection and respect displayed by pupils is the result of emotional difficulties of which they are victim, and their wish to be 'recognized' in spite of their weakness at school. It is hard to underestimate the significance of the emotional bonding between teachers and taught, young people and adults, particularly in schools considered difficult. This probably applies more to lower-secondary than upper-secondary schooling. In this respect, the transfer to the *lycée* is a critical point at which adolescents have the impression they are cast adrift because they feel less supervised. In *lycées*, pupils feel more anonymous and are therefore more likely to consider they are not respected. During their initial training, teachers should have been led to understand this need for outward self-expression on the part of pupils who may feel 'lost' at the *lycée*. Such pupils – and this point has to be stressed during initial training or courses for would-be teachers – tolerate neither disregard nor familiarity towards themselves on the part of adults. At the same time, they do not consider themselves bound to these adults by any sense of obligation, except those who, because of their attitude or work, have managed to command respect.

The relationship with families

The 'abdication' of families

The expression 'abdication of responsibility' is often used in the developed countries to describe the attitude of parents. It seems that, in schools considered difficult, families expect that the institution should provide everything, including the authority and influence that they are unable to exert over their children. Yet parents are always absent from meetings dealing with their children's progress. Thus an apparently total lack of interest exists alongside complete confidence in the school concerned. Such is the paradoxical attitude of parents who often have no family tradition of sustained study, and may themselves have often failed at school.

Teachers thus have to realize that families do not find it easy to visit their children's schools; and that teaching staff in general often feel they are inconveniencing families when informing them about their children's prolonged absence, or some incident of which they may have been victim. Meanwhile, families are demanding 'consumers', totally unwilling to discuss matters reasonably when teachers or others presume to 'judge' their children, or strive to compensate for their own negligence. Yet the family environment exerts a considerable influence on the behaviour of children. Teachers can gauge for themselves the harmful effects where there is no firm parental control, or where adults offer a negative role model. Trends in family structures, for example as a result of divorce or the existence of single-parent families, often mean that parents are overburdened by (both financial and emotional) responsibilities, while their children are uncertain of their identity.

Airing of all such aspects in pre-service or in-service training may help to overcome "the reluctance of teachers to meet families that are suspected of being educationally inadequate" (Slawski and Scherer, 1979). For teachers are on occasions somewhat suspicious of families, as pointed out in the following document adopted at the end of 1994 by the European Trade Union Committee for Education (ETUCE): "the parents must be fully involved as partners, although recognizing that in some cases parental or cultural attitudes engendered through the family could create difficulties for students and their teachers" (ETUCE/CSEE, 1994, p. 70).

The relationship of families and schools is paradoxical. When pupils are from comfortable backgrounds and get on at school, parents are very determined to be involved in their children's progress there, in a way that teachers often find hard to accept. On the other hand, where the situation has deteriorated and/or school failure is widespread, the presence of parents in the school is very strongly recommended by all partners since it seems vital. Yet the families who get involved in this case are few. In France, the result is that the participation rate of parents in *collège* board elections is much lower at ZEP institutions. In 1996-97, in the Val de Marne *département* to the south of Paris, this rate was 15 per cent for ZEP *collèges* compared to 27 per cent at *collèges* elsewhere.

Mediators have been employed to encourage dialogue between teachers and disadvantaged families that are unaccustomed to visiting their children's school and often apprehensive about the idea. Other initiatives have been launched because the presence and involvement of families regarding school greatly increases their children's own prospects there: "In some cases, a pupil's report will be handed over in person to families who have made the effort to come to the school or *collège*, and who will take the opportunity to speak to the principal teacher. In others, *collège* activities arranged for local women will enable them to get to know the headteacher" (Auduc, 1996).

"To make it easier to become acquainted with others, a collège in Alsace laid on culinary specialities from different countries and regions on three separate Saturdays. The meals were prepared by the mothers of pupils, with the assistance of several associations. The pupils brought photographs, cakes and many other specialities from their countries of origin ... This provided an opportunity to see at the school parents who never came to meetings ... Since this initiative, there has been a very significant impact on dialogue with the families: relations have been considerably improved, especially with the parents who were involved in the cooking." (Council of Europe, 1997).

Co-operation with families

In most European countries, the role of families in school management is essentially consultative. The purpose of partnerships between families and institutions in disadvantaged urban areas is to encourage parents to become more active and involved in school life. The extent to which they participate varies in accordance with the degree to which schools are autonomous. It is considerable in countries such as the United Kingdom, Denmark, Spain and Portugal.

Schemes in the **United Kingdom** have sought to encourage families to play a fuller part in some school activities. Thus in Coventry, during a campaign to boost reading ability, families became involved in classroom work and, as a result, were able to observe their children's activities. Under these circumstances, the teachers advised them how to help with their children's schoolwork. Lending libraries or school reading areas are made available to them (Walker, 1992) so that families might encourage their children to read

The Project funded by the Van Leer Foundation in **Ireland**, grants parents a key role in the implementation of specific measures to address underachievement at school in the badly disadvantaged urban area of Rutland Street. In 1991, the Irish Ministry of Education distributed a questionnaire, in which he warmly encouraged action related to this initiative, on the part of parents' associations (Payet and Van Zantem, 1996).

School absenteeism

School absenteeism is an endemic misfortune in schools with an intake considered difficult. All-out effort by teams of educators manages to bring it under control through extensive regular follow-up, thanks in particular to an increase in the number of monitors. Absenteeism is attributable to many different causes ranging from the fact that, in families where no one is at work in the morning, 'nobody wakes up', to a simple desire to do something else.

Furthermore, surveys in France have revealed that the proportion of children eating in the school cafeteria was generally very low at institutions in ZEPs or 'sensitive' areas, primarily for financial reasons. In this country, the Ministry of Education considers that "the rate of cafeteria attendance seems to be the main distinguishing criterion in drawing up a typology of 'sensitive' institutions particularly in that, within most of them, canteen attendance is steadily falling. In all *collèges*, 60.1 per cent of pupils take school meals, 32 per cent take school meals in urban ZEPs and 22.3 per cent in *collèges* classified as 'sensitive''' (Braunstein and Dasté, 1994, p. 17). Appropriate remedial action – such as that of subsidizing school meals – is the responsibility of the planner and the politician. But, here again, teachers must be forewarned about this situation.

Achieving a good atmosphere inside a school

To conclude the present chapter, it is worth noting the criteria enumerated by Jacques Hebert regarding a good school atmosphere:

- the importance attached to learning and knowledge;
- teaching organized in a way that encourages staff to give of their best;
- responsible participation by pupils in school life;
- staff able to demonstrate an adult behavioural model to pupils;
- leadership in teaching activity and methods on the part of school management;
- parental participation in school business;
- material conditions indicative of an orderly school (Hebert, 1991).

Clearly, all these aims cannot be dealt with at a single attempt during training. But is it possible to educate, without indulging in dreams and a measure of idealism?

V. Preparing for teamwork, and internal and external partnership for teaching in 'difficult urban areas'

Making experience of schools considered difficult, a compulsory part of training

Class management may certainly be learned by means of simulation exercises and practical lessons, but it is more important to gain direct classroom experience during practice teaching. When trainees have an opportunity to observe the complexity of classroom situations, to talk them over with the teacher responsible for the class, and to assume responsibility for the same class, under the supervision of that teacher, their approach to problems becomes more effective.

As a 1994 French Ministry of Education report puts it: "'sensitive' institutions, and/or those in ZEPs, should be compulsory training grounds for our future teachers. There, they will discover a real dimension of the education system, in which they themselves will at some stage be involved. They will include teams of educators as a rule more generous, more welcoming and with a greater sense of solidarity than elsewhere. Many trainee teachers may even come to prefer such schools".

The importance of the tutor's role

In forging professional identity, training by more experienced peers has a specific and unique part to play. The role of such tutors is important for all trainee teachers, regardless of the kind of school in which they are going to teach. But it is even more essential for those who are going to work in institutions considered difficult. Working alongside these tutor/teachers, they will be able to discover that it is possible to pursue one's occupation and get pupils to do well in situations which, at first sight, appear delicate – matters that cause anxiety among beginners. Tutors who supervise new teachers, besides having a sound command of knowledge relevant to their school subject and the ability to teach it well, are also trainers who have thought extensively about ways of communicating knowledge and know-how to their peers, even where the latter are beginners.

The key role of the tutor has been recognized in **England and Wales**, with the development of mentors. The use of mentors is a very conspicuous new feature of the partnerships which have long existed between university-based teacher training and schools. The idea is to concentrate trainees in some schools that so wish, in order that they may be involved for much longer in the activity and life of a school, working there with mentors. The latter are not meant to demonstrate what they do in the classroom, but to help beginners analyze methods, seek relevant professional information and advise them on professional questions.

In 1992, the British Ministry of Education decided that at least two-thirds of time devoted to teacher training should be spent within schools, which represented an increase of over 30 per cent. Thus, a school/mentor partnership takes charge of the entire process from the initial lesson planning to final student assessment. In the system of 'School-based pre-service teacher training', newcomers are trained for their occupational duties:

- by observing lessons given by experienced teachers who demonstrate what they are doing;
- by benefiting from a mentor at the school, who acts as trainer.

Such a system may soon entirely replace traditional teacher training courses offered by universities in the final year of training.

The school as a place for training

The United Kingdom is not the only country in which an important part of the teacher training takes place in schools. In most countries, the position of practical work involving contact with pupils in a school occupies between a third and a half of the time spent in the last two years of pre-service training.

In the **USA**, the transformation of a number of schools into Schools for Professional Development, along the lines of university hospitals for medical students, has been advocated. In such schools, teaching takes place alongside training teachers to conduct research in university-based programmes, for the simultaneous teaching of pupils, and the training of future teachers for research.

In **Italy** and **Greece**, school-based courses for trainees have developed markedly since the start of the 1990s.

In **Austria**, the Minister of Education stated in 1993 that the programme of pre-service teacher training should include a theoretical part and also practical training in class management. The latter includes visits and study of teaching methods, along with classroom exercises involving learning strategies intended to create a positive classroom climate and resolve awkward situations.

In **France**, courses are included in the second year of the University Teacher Training Institutes (the IUFMs), after the competitive entrance examination has been successfully completed. Conducted by a tutor/adviser on teaching practice, they are equivalent to one-third of a year's professional teaching. Separate practice teaching takes place involving 40 hours in schools at other levels of education.

Specific training for work with disadvantaged pupils may take the form of:

* training modules for the teaching of such pupils;
* courses in 'sensitive' or ZEP schools, conducted by advisers on teaching practice who work in these schools.

In **Belgium**, the Ministry has introduced a modular system into pre-service training, which includes courses in disadvantaged environments and preparation for intercultural education.

In **Germany**, lessons in class management, problem resolution and group dynamics, though generally very widespread, are not compulsory.

In **Norway**, in both lower secondary and primary education, a theoretical and practical working programme in teaching practice entitled 'Understanding pupils and looking after them' is included in the curriculum.

Teamwork and teacher co-operation: crucial aspects of their profession

In schools considered difficult, teamwork is more frequent and important than elsewhere. Teachers are less isolated in their occupation, and more convinced of the benefits of teamwork for boosting pupil attainment. They are also led, more than elsewhere, to work with colleagues and partners outside their school.

Reduced occupational isolation

In difficult schools, teachers who are confronted with innumerable daily problems, repeatedly asked about their teaching methods, and concerned by developments outside their school, all have to adopt, to some extent, a team approach in place of their individualistic coping strategies. Naturally, this may vary with respect to the country or school concerned, since the charisma of management staff, the specifics and history of each school, and the individual career paths of its leading actors are also relevant factors. Yet the net result is always a more credible educational community which is inclined to greater solidarity and more active than elsewhere, with a sense that its work and very survival depend on this commitment.

Rather than deriving solely from daily contact with pupils, the identity of new teachers is also a product of their role in a team of similarly placed colleagues, with whom they must plan work in accordance with their novel obligations. The team constantly investigates ways of adapting teaching to children's environment and cultures as effectively as possible. The need for an educational team has become increasingly self-evident in all schools with large numbers of disadvantaged pupils, under pressure from two main factors:

- the kind of teaching required by such pupils: assistance with learning becomes more relevant and effective where it is based on co-operation and the combined potential of an entire team;
- local needs, which cannot all be managed at a distance from a central administrative source.

Teachers work with various social actors in a partnership calling for new skills that have to be acquired during pre-service teacher training:

- organization of group work;
- reasoned defence of team decisions;
- ability to negotiate as well as advise and inform;
- preparing schemes;
- seeking resources.

Teacher teamwork

From being an individualized occupation which was pursued mainly within the confines of a classroom or office, teaching is becoming a relational, public profession directly influenced by local issues. Instead of being simply an institutional obligation, teamwork is the best form of protection against difficulties encountered in daily occupational practice. It can help teachers to beat 'teacher burnout' – that body of symptoms linked to weariness and a sense of exhaustion resulting from the need to ceaselessly nourish young minds.

In **France**, the vast majority of teachers assigned classes that are considered difficult say they work actively with both colleagues in their discipline, and those who have the same class. Work in these classes means a greater amount of time devoted to preparing lessons, corrections, homework and exercises. It would seem, therefore, that workload increases in difficult schools and classes while, at the same time, the range of professional skills becomes broader as tasks get more diversified to include:

- material tasks: organizing the working area, preparing documents and using technical equipment;

- symbolic tasks: communicating, analyzing and reshaping ideas, and considering possible kinds of support for learning;
- cognitive tasks: observing class activity, and interpreting and assessing pupil performance;
- emotional behaviour and aggressiveness, steering and controlling group behaviour.

Teachers who work in difficult classes consider that conditions there oblige them to undertake additional training.

Partnership with local actors

In many countries, partnership involves mobilizing various agencies, including local associations, social workers and firms, on behalf of a school. This energy generated around schools in their support to pupils with their homework can galvanize the action of professional educators.

The programme for social reform in the **Netherlands** provides for partnership agreements between municipalities and schools that can draw on a local fund to tackle problems at school, such as premature pupil drop-out. 'School attendance committees' have been set up in some municipalities and regions to reduce drop-out and absenteeism from school.

Municipalities and schools join forces in many local ventures especially to give impetus to compensatory educational initiatives for pupils from disadvantaged neighbourhoods:

- in **Portugal** and **Spain**, priority action is targeted at the children of nomadic groups or seasonal workers;
- **Italy** takes preventive action against drug-abuse;
- in **France,** external groups help with remedial work and homework;
- in **Germany**, firms and regional authorities are both very active in the fight against school failure. The *Länder* grant financial support to firms which train young people underachieving at school;

- in the **Netherlands**, some firms partner technical schools in schemes for the professional, social and scholastic reintegration of young people who have dropped out.

Developing multiple teaching skills and methods

Teachers believe that the most efficient technique is work in small groups combined with teaching adapted to suit pupils of varied ability. In this context, the use of graded exercises is the most common procedure. The recommendation in official programmes (particularly those in France, the Netherlands and Spain) that teaching should be adjusted to pupil requirements is essential. Many schools, however, engage in internal streaming of pupils according to some measure of their ability. Furthermore, young people must acquire autonomous learning skills. Consequently, teachers who have completed their training should be able, in collaboration with the school documentation centre or library and its specialist staff, to teach a child to take notes, consult a dictionary or a file index, and draw up an outline. For example, the history curriculum in the French Community of Belgium states that pupils must learn 'to handle a book, and consult a table of contents or an index'.

Projects linking entry to the labour market, social integration and education

It appears important to inform first-time teachers about teaching initiatives conducted by staff in difficult schools and/or classes, such as schemes to prevent young people in serious difficulty from avoiding school. Some of these initiatives are aimed at enabling young people to gain the knowledge required for the award of a professional qualification with its diploma, to assimilate business-related skills or to secure their entry on to the labour market. In some cases, a teacher is appointed as 'pupil co-ordinator'. In others, formal last-chance arrangements for the most difficult cases are introduced, under which a contract is concluded with pupils who have four months to complete their own individual study plan. The timetable has three equally weighted elements, namely training, sport and culture, and economic and social information. With strong input from the sociomedical sector, it is intended to combine social and professional integration with concern for appropriate education.

In another school, alternation between studies and practical work offers a future to very seriously handicapped pupils. Teachers encourage the participation of parents and external partners in helping the young people to 'find a way forward'.

Making the most of experience to date

'Circumstances that one normally expects to be the most difficult, whether in Harlem or Franc-Moisin, are also those that force schools to act'. These were the words used by *Libération* on 28 March 1995 to refer to a meeting at Saint-Denis, France, organized to consider the experimental activity of the New York Central Park East Secondary School (CPESS) and the Saint-Denis *Auto-École* (school for autonomous learning).

The heads of these schools "for pupils who are failing dramatically" (*Le Monde*, 29 March 1995) feel they have in common "the determination never to give up when confronted with failure, as well as their location in a difficult environment". Teachers in both schools have volunteered to work in them, and agreed to abide by their principles.

The New York CPEES has been in existence for 10 years, and is the focus of a vast network for school reform. It has an intake of 450 pupils from a class level equivalent to the French *sixième* (pupils aged around 12) upwards, and each teacher tutors a group of 15. Weekly meetings for teachers are open to parents and pupil councils. The teachers decide on the curriculum, rules, diplomas and even daily class routine. The basic teaching principle is 'less is more' adopted from an interdisciplinary standpoint with respect for the curriculum, but in accordance with each group of pupils' particular pace.

The Saint-Denis school for autonomous learning has existed since 1995 for around 30 pupils excluded from normal schooling. With appropriately tailored tutorial-based teaching methods, it attempts to rehabilitate them in one, or sometimes two years. Boys and girls work independently, in accordance with objective-based learning in which teachers offer individually adapted guidance, making each pupil responsible for his or her own progress.

In the **United Kingdom**, 47 Local Education Authorities (LEA) possess community schools, and there are now 750 community colleges. Community education seeks to mobilize teams of supervisors and educators who work with young people in schools or local premises. Its aim is to forestall or reduce the impact of exclusion, through developing the practical, cognitive and moral education of young people at risk. Among these initiatives are the following:

- general training and education programmes in schools, colleges and vocational training institutions;
- alternative projects conducted by young people themselves, in liaison with local associations;
- partnerships between various services and occupations involving representatives from the public, private and voluntary sectors, whose activities have an impact on the life of young people in difficulty.

Under the 'My career' programme in **Finland**, a comprehensive school for young people allergic to school has been set up in Tekeva. Its aim is to help them position themselves in the 'no man's land' between school and work. The arrangement is intended for pupils in the last two years of compulsory school (at the age of 15 or 16) who display negative attitudes (aggressive behaviour, absenteeism, etc.) towards school. Study at a place of work is alternated with study in small groups so that the young people can subsequently gain access to provision for vocational training.

As part of the new programme for final-year secondary education in **Sweden**, a scheme has been created for young people of *lycée* level who are in difficulty. Each young person concerned negotiates a study plan with the Youth Guidance service. This plan lays down the period of study and has to include practical work in each subject. The scheme aims to motivate the young people and prepare them to enter mainstream training.

In **Italy**, a school in Tuscany is committed to fighting 'the anxiety of young people'. The initiative includes training research courses for them, as well as parents or teachers, with the aim of diagnosing jointly the anxiety experienced by the young. A reception centre has been set up within the school.

In **Germany** the *Land* (State) of Berlin set up an association for young people who had left compulsory schooling, where they had an opportunity to gain practical experience in different training centres. In 1992, this project became a public experimental school, in which pupils unsuited to traditional schooling could complete their ninth and tenth years of compulsory schooling and obtain a school diploma.

Several schemes seek to provide second-chance schooling to fight exclusion, by making use of new teaching methods, information technologies and multimedia.

In **France**, the 'open school' project offers holiday-period activities in an initiative run by each school in disadvantaged areas. "Recent experience proves that the image of school is enhanced both among young people and local residents. The school reasserts its legitimacy for them. For these pupils, the project represents a step forward in the re-establishment of their normal school status, as they accept once more the rules governing collective life there" (Fotinos and Poupelin, 1995).

These and many other experiments are of unquestionable interest and future teachers, in all countries, should be fully aware of their significance. They show how schools have decided to deal unequivocally with all aspects of educating difficult pupils. In some respects, this tends to generate fresh confidence in schools and their mission. Such an optimistic finding gives good grounds for tackling the problems posed by those pupils, and overcoming what teachers think are the hardest objectives to achieve, namely interesting the least motivated and getting mixed-ability pupils to work together.

Taking account of pupils and giving them a sense of responsibility

Studies carried out in France show that the teachers with the most negative perception of their pupils are those who work in schools classified as having a 'difficult intake' (in ZEPs or 'sensitive' areas). Most of them agree that "only children sure to succeed should have access to schools" implying "early selection and orientation towards shorter forms of secondary schooling that are less optimistic about pupil potential if not actually rigid in determining pupil fate at an early age". (Ministry of Education, Direction de l'Évaluation et de la Prospective, 1994, p. 72). These teachers thus disagree with the aim of educating a generation of pupils as long as possible. Attributable to the difficulties they encounter in their classes, their attitudes demonstrate how important it is that they should consider the question of a 'greater sense of responsibility for pupils' from the outset, in their training.

If young people are made to feel more responsible, it is easier for them to develop an independent personalized approach to their work. Learning about citizenship and responsibility has to be a gradual process from primary to upper-secondary education. When pupils exercise their rights and, conversely, respect their obligations at all stages of schooling, they become accustomed to assuming responsibility, while their relations with the rest of the school community are more readily transformed. In schools considered difficult, this approach is even more important, in demonstrating how rights and obligations govern the workings of a school. The rights of pupils to meet, to form associations, to be informed, and to prepare newsletters amount to a set of rules that should be respected by all members of the educational community. Similarly, each pupil should respect the dignity of his or her peers as well as that of adults in the school.

If anyone breaches this social and moral contract, law becomes non-existent, with a real attendant risk of excesses and the emergence of aggressive behaviour. Teachers therefore have to accept the basic importance of developing the citizenship of young people, particularly through encouraging pupils to assume real responsibility.

Adapting curricula to school realities

Adaptation of national curricula with due regard for the requirements of pupils and their individual circumstances is a policy implemented in many countries for autonomous schools. It needs to be considered in teacher training.

School-based schemes

In **France**, the July 1989 Orientation Law stated that all schools had to draw up a school plan approved by their governing board for the purpose of adapting education to pupil diversity, with due respect for national texts and curricula. The pedagogical aspects of the plan had to be prepared by the teaching staff.

In the **Netherlands**, each school has a school plan. In **Italy**, each *scuola média* has to establish an annual plan setting out its purpose and aims, and providing remedial assistance to pupils in difficulty. Relations between schools with a difficult intake and their local environment result in urban area or district plans.

The **United Kingdom** community schools are linked to their local environment in their architectural conception, especially as regards their sports and classroom facilities, meeting rooms, and areas for exhibitions or documentation centres, open to pupils as well as adults. The learning and attitudes inculcated by the school have to be put into practice in all these activities. In this way, pupils may have opportunities to discover fresh motivation or forms of help they might need.

Remedial education measures

Pupils from disadvantaged areas require more help than others in their schoolwork. Trainee teachers have to be aware of the need to offer specific kinds of assistance to pupils. This assistance can be offered within the school by teachers or supervisors in the form of remedial lessons, tutorials or supervised study. It may also be an opportunity for partnership between a school and local student association, pensioners, or municipalities, like the partnership programmes referred to above. These kinds of collaboration have to be foreseen by teachers as part of their plan, so that the different inputs involved are truly complementary, and not competitive or in conflict.

Taking account of all work done by schools in their evaluation

In schools with an intake considered difficult, it is quite clear that straightforward conventional teaching is not enough, and has to be supplemented by numerous initiatives mobilizing the entire environment around the school. A problem arises in annual evaluation of these programmes when the examination results are almost the only means of assessment. The annual cycle of results and, with it, the resources allocated, do not provide for sufficiently sustained examination of the work carried out. Three-year minimum contracts are desirable to ensure the stability of staff and resources, in which case results would be assessed at the end of the contract.

Furthermore, the findings are not always encouraging, because they are linked solely to school results in which progress depends on changes of attitude on the part of pupils, which are not easy to detect. In taking account exclusively of conventional examination results and not an improved school atmosphere – which is eventually a factor in improved knowledge acquisition – the operational costs of programmes in schools whose pupil intake is considered difficult, may be very high for only a modest return. This criticism has often been expressed in England and Wales with regard to the Low Attainments Pupils Programme (LAPP).

VI. Responding to the challenges: enabling teachers to succeed; restoring meaning to school

Restoring meaning to current teaching practice

Working in schools where most pupils are in difficulty, may be an incomparable way of highlighting plainly what is crucial, and restoring meaning to current teaching practice.

Although most countries have today become aware of the need to offer teachers a sound training in their discipline, they are only just beginning to appreciate the importance of training them in teaching methods that will lead them to understand the learning difficulties of pupils.

In **Denmark**, **Portugal** and the **Netherlands**, future teachers are directly initiated into the problems of pupils having difficulty with their mother tongue and mathematics.

Scotland has created a specific diploma for 'Education of pupils with learning difficulties' awarded by a teacher-training institute.

Since the May 1996 circulars in **France**, the IUFMs prepare future teachers to practise in a variety of circumstances, some of them difficult, with the possibility that they might encounter aggressiveness, conflict and perhaps violence. The content of this training includes the following:

- meetings with school teams confronted by difficult situations;
- trainee periods as observers in difficult classes, which are prepared and used in workshops on professional situations and methods.

Themes considered include pupils in difficulty, conflict, refusal to work, aggressive behaviour, high-risk behaviour (tobacco, alcoholism, drugs), cultural diversity and the health of young people.

In other countries, the foregoing themes are covered during in-service training. In **Germany**, depending on the *Land*, there is training in conflict prevention. In **Greece** every two years, teachers have to undergo a three-month period of training devoted to new teaching methods. In **Portugal**, the 'educational curriculum for all' has led to the establishment of the resource centre for schooling 'in the year 2000', which is responsible for training to prevent school drop-out. **Luxembourg** is implementing a training programme to introduce strategies for differentiated teaching.

While it is clear that these kinds of training occur essentially in the industrialized countries, their introduction will soon be on the agenda of all others worldwide.

What should be the content of training?

As we have seen in the preceding chapters, teachers need to acquire a wide range of skills. The teacher of the twenty-first century will have to know how to do the following:

- organize a teaching plan;
- prepare and implement a learning situation and evaluate it;
- manage relational phenomena;
- teach study skills to pupils;
- encourage the growth of positive professional aspirations;
- work with partners.

When they practise these skills, teachers mobilize knowledge in three fields for which it is crucial that they be trained:

- those concerning the subject matter: subject content to be taught, and the history, epistemology and social implications of different disciplines;

- those concerned with the management of learning (whether didactic or pedagogical);
- those concerning the education system: national educational practice, structure and function of schools, understanding the dynamics of school-based schemes.

Training should, therefore, possess the following methodologies:

- an approach centred on the young person concerned: cognitive, economic, psychological and social development;
- the concept of the teamwork approach;
- learning theories;
- the teacher as someone responsible for curricular content;
- application of research results;
- intercultural education;
- equality of opportunity and respect for democratic values;
- the horizontal approach to educational problems: relations, behaviour and evaluation;
- teaching methods for different age groups: children, adolescents, adults.

Knowledge linked to teaching practice should cover the ability to:

- communicate with pupils, teachers, other members of staff and parents;
- take an interest in children and their potential for learning in a given social and cultural context.

Teacher training has to be such as to enable understanding of how knowledge is selected, organized and transmitted. The main questions related to effective working practice that can be raised in training, may include:

- how should one analyze the environment in which a school is situated?
- what is the underlying purpose of teaching at the school?
- how does the educational team operate?
- how are relations with families organized?

115

- what are the school's relations with other schools in the town or city, or with its potential partners?

Alongside essential training centred on subject-related skills, teacher training should, in particular, extend to the psychology, teaching skills or social sciences which underpin essential abilities in analysis and communication. It also has to include an introduction to the management of group dynamics (especially training in conflict resolution), as well as in project-based learning, in helping pupils achieve their own personal objectives and in implementation of goals concerned with solidarity, methods and citizenship. Intercultural education also has to be a principle underlying teacher training. And given conditions in schools considered difficult, both didactic and practical lessons in class management and interpersonal relations clearly have to be included in training.

Because of the difficulties of going straight into teaching for the first time, with entire responsibility for a class, especially in a school considered difficult, it is advisable to lighten the workload during the first full year of activity, however good initial training may have been. In this way, new teachers can get the benefit of specific monitoring – a kind of selective continuous training to meet their needs as determined by occupational circumstances, including the school with disadvantaged pupils, cultural diversity, violence and so forth. "Entry into the profession should no longer be considered as a sort of initiation rite during which it is necessary to suffer and to demonstrate one's stamina as has happened in the past" (ETUCE/CSEE, 1994).

Pre-service training must be considered the basis for a process of continuity to stimulate a growing demand for in-service training. Indeed, there has to be substantial consistency between pre-service training and in-service training, both of which should be founded on the same guiding principles. Given the rapidity of change, teaching, more than any other profession, needs constantly to adjust the knowledge on which it is based, whether academic or related to practical, cultural or social aspects. Pre-service training is not enough to guarantee the expertise required throughout an entire career, and in-service training is essential in developing the necessary skills. With this in mind, higher education institutions have to develop educational research programmes directly applicable to pre-service and in-service training, reflecting and influencing real classroom methods employed in different school environments.

How are staff to be encouraged to teach in schools located in urban areas considered difficult?

In the overwhelming majority of cases, teaching staff in schools considered difficult are young, without much experience and sometimes in situations of precarious employment. Difficulty in securing stable staffing for management, teaching and administration – with relatively high rates of resignation or refusal to accept posts, and a substantial rate of transfer elsewhere at the end of a single year – compromise the possibility of providing multi-annual continuity in team or institutional plan. This inability to plan ahead is liable to compromise pupil attainment. Thus, a variety of different measures have been envisaged to encourage staff to volunteer for work in schools of this kind, including financial bonuses and easier transfers elsewhere after three years' service.

An experiment is under way in an IUFM in the eastern suburbs of Paris in which there are many schools considered difficult. Launched with secondary education teachers, it is to be gradually extended to teachers in primary education where fairly similar problems arise. Following the introduction in 1994, of the possibility of assigning teachers to so-called 'sensitive' schools if they so request, the Creteil *Académie* IUFM decided to locate practice teaching in these schools, with the right, again if trainees so wished, to be permanently posted in them at the end of the year. This option is based on the principle that, given the teaching conditions in such schools, a slight jolt during practice teaching supervised by an advisory tutor is preferable to a full-scale baptism of fire with no support whatever during a first-time career assignment. The staff concerned benefit from specific training for teaching pupils considered difficult, called 'Teaching in Suburbs', throughout the entire school year.

In 1994, 27 per cent of trainees across all disciplines who undertook this practice teaching requested that they remain in their 'sensitive' school. In 1995, the corresponding figure was 33 per cent. Among the reasons put forward for their request were the following:

- being a teacher is 'more useful' and 'more effective' with young people from disadvantaged areas;
- the attractiveness of teamwork within these schools and the quality of relations within the teams, the wish to take part in a school-based teaching plan, and in teamwork;
- the specific modules organized for them: 'Teaching in Suburbs' helped them to develop a more positive view of problems posed by young people;
- personal familiarity with disadvantaged milieux, prior experience acquired with adolescents during work with associations;
- "pupils in my *lycée,* a 'sensitive' school, show a real need. Such relations are stimulating, in spite of the difficulties ....";
- "I wish to make a serious effort in helping young people from these areas to do well at school, while drawing on the social, geographical and historical heritage surrounding them, with which I am familiar";
- the enhanced work of the teacher who succeeds in the fight against school failure;
- "difficulties encountered during practice teaching in a 'sensitive' *lycée* helped me to develop my thoughts as a teacher about compensating for shortcomings at school in both the specific mathematics curriculum, and the mathematical tools used by pupils in other subjects";
- "for young people in 'sensitive' schools, history and geography may contribute to better mastery of their social environment, better understanding of the world they live in, and successful integration within society";
- "it is in this kind of school that the real challenge of education lies".

A few guidelines for effective professionalization of teachers

Preparation of teachers to manage their classes, secure compromises, use instructive digressions, devise pathways and plan for the consecutive stages of teaching – in short, to be creative, with precise strategies for classroom learning – should probably involve training lasting four semesters. This training might be devised as follows:

*First semester: concerned with **occupational adaptation***

This period would essentially involve, on the one hand, teaching practice in schools with a very diverse pupil intake, so that future teachers might observe and become familiar with occupational practice, alongside more experienced teachers; and, on the other, sessions focused on the theory and practice of teaching in the one or more subjects concerned. The aim of this provision would be to establish ongoing interaction between trainees and experienced teachers working in classes considered difficult.

Attention would be paid to actually experienced difficulties. While these difficulties would be initially viewed in terms of lack of discipline and aggressive behaviour on the part of pupils, which raise issues concerned with rules or punishment, problems regarding the conception and conduct of the successive stages of teaching activity, as well as the acquisition of knowledge by pupils, would also be examined, since they too are factors in classroom unrest.

*Second semester: concerned with **methods analysis***

This period would primarily include some hours of actual teaching carried out by the trainee, with responsibility for one or several classes under the guidance of a teacher acting as an adviser on practice. Trainees would have to draft a professional report based on analysis of the teaching methods employed during their different teaching practice experiences. Their continued training and first-time appointment as teachers would depend on an assessment of their

119

ability. During the first two semesters, training sessions, and joint deliberation involving first-time teachers, trainers and teaching advisers would focus on several approaches. Issues to be examined might include the following:

♦ *How should a school be diagnosed? What indicators are useful?*

- What are the characteristics of its pupils?
- Among its pupils, what proportion are from disadvantaged socio-professional categories, grant-holders, pupils of foreign origin or from ethnic minorities, or having repeated more than two years of schooling?
- The school in the image of its environment: are the school, *collège* or *lycée* concerned totally representative of their surrounding neighbourhood, or do they enrol solely pupils from its most impoverished sector?
- Class composition: how is mixed-ability and attitudes handled at school?
- Policy for pupil orientation: how do teachers perform assessment? Are pupils whose results are low allowed to go on to the next grade?
- Is the school akin to an enclave?
- What is the teaching-staff turnover?
- What are the relations with parents? How are they to be situated? Are they only apparent when there are problems? What kind of communication exists? Is negotiation possible?

♦ *What is the partnership with the environment?*

- What assistance with homework and reading, etc. is provided in the school?
- Which local actors can lend their support to the tasks of teachers?

♦ *What relationship does the pupil have with learning?*

- How does one define a pupil 'in difficulty'?

- How are absenteeism and refusals to work managed?

- What remedial action is possible: tutoring, 'contract' teaching, differentiated teaching methods, etc.?

♦ *How does one analyze aggressive behaviour by pupils?*

- How should management of fear and aggressiveness be learned?
- How are staff alerted to the fact that some pupils perceive attitudes not corresponding to their own norms as acts of violence?
- What should be the relations with police/the judicial authorities and the national education ministry?
- What are the characteristics of high-risk behaviour, what action should be taken against drug abuse?

♦ *What should constitute education for citizenship?*

- What are the concepts of limit, right and law?
- How are internal regulations to be drawn up?
- How does one educate for a sense of individual and collective responsibility?
- How does one educate to form judgements, and to listen to others?

♦ *What kind of occupation should teaching now be?*

- How should teamwork be managed at school?
- What is the ethical and civic dimension of teaching?
- What are the rights and duties of teachers?

*Third semester: concerned with **adaptation for the job***

First-time teachers would work half-time in the schools to which they were posted. Alongside them would be an experienced teacher playing the part of a tutor who would help them, support them and enable them to discover the school, its pupils, the local environment, etc. New teachers would thus become directly and rapidly familiar with all aspects of the teaching team, and work with their tutor on subjects such as scholastic assessment, marking work by pupils, the successive stages of teaching and establishing class rules. If need be, they would be able to voice all difficulties, anxieties, and doubts as soon as they surfaced. Beginners might also visit classes taken by their tutor who, in turn, might come to the classes being given by his or her colleague in the first year.

If important issues were to come to light regarding difficulties in class management, methods analysis groups might be formed around trainers, new teachers who volunteered and more experienced colleagues. The aim of this third semester would be to allow teachers to manage the time needed to become really familiar with the school in which they were posted, its local environment, and pupil characteristics, while giving them the opportunity, with support from a tutor, to develop responses, experiment with them during their classes and evaluate them individually or collectively.

*Fourth semester: concerned with **involvement in a team***

New teachers, in liaison with teacher-counsellors would take part in a plan, an initiative or an activity calling for teamwork. This might involve:

- the duties of principal teacher or activity co-ordinator in primary schooling;
- the establishment of tutorials;
- an interdisciplinary teaching project;
- monitoring the activity of clubs or associations within the school.

In order to secure permanent tenured status, new teachers should submit a monitoring report on this activity. During this period, provision might be made for courses lasting several days, attended by teachers and other players active in the local environment of the school. Far from involving solely those professions accustomed to working with young people at school, these joint initiatives might mobilize all those whose responsibilities and tasks lead them to work with disadvantaged people. They would encourage first-time teachers to think more about their occupation, their role and the meaning of school.

The stage-by-stage provision of this kind of training based on adaptation to the job and the occupation, as well as on accompanying support from experienced teachers throughout the two years, would avoid the sharp contrast experienced by newcomers between their impression, when students, of teaching, and the realities of the field in practice.

Restoring a sense of purpose to the teaching profession

Training teachers to work in schools and/or classes considered difficult is thus a challenge commensurate with the needs of our times. Teachers may discover a new sense of responsibility in the following:

- Ensuring that schools are places where knowledge is acquired, and where the study of no field of learning is ruled out, so that critical thinking on the part of young people is encouraged.

- Ensuring that schools are places for learning the values of generosity, solidarity and democracy, and for the development of citizenship.

In short, teachers can help young people to enter "a society made for school and not a school made for society", in accordance with the wish expressed by Gaston Bachelard.

Bibliography

Abdallah-Preyceille, M. 1992. *Quelle école pour quelle intégration ?*, Centre national de documentation pédagogique, Paris: Hachette.

Anderson, D.S. 1974. *L'acquisition d'une identité professionnelle chez les élèves professeurs*, Paris: OECD.

Arora, R.; Duncan, C. (eds.). 1986. *Multicultural education towards good practice.* London: Routledge and Kegan Paul.

Auduc, J.-L. 1994. *Le Système éducatif français.* Paris: Hachette.

Auduc, J.-L. 1996. *Enseigner en "Banlieues"* Paris: Hachette.

Becker, H. 1983. "Studying urban schools". In: *Anthropology and Education Quarterly.* Vol. 14(2).

Black, H. 1993. *Enseigner et certification, étude de cas écossaise.* Strasbourg: Council of Europe.

Body-Gendrot, S. 1991. *Les Etats-Unis et leurs immigrants. Des modes d'insertion variés.* Paris:La Documentation Française.

Braustein, M.; Dasté, P. 1994. *Rapport sur le fonctionnement des établissements sensibles.* Paris: Ministère de l'Education nationale.

Brittan, E. 1976. "Multi-racial education, teacher opinion on aspects of school life (2): Pupils and Teachers". In: *Educational Research.* Vol. 18 (3).

Centre de recherches tsiganes, *Interface*, Bulletin d'Information. Paris:Université René Descartes.

Centre national de documentation pédagogique (CNDP). 1994. *Education à la paix.* Paris.

Charlot, B. 1997. *Du rapport au savoir, éléments pour une théorie.* Paris: Anthropos.

Charlot, B.; Bautier, E.; Rochex, J.-Y. 1993. *Ecole et Savoir dans les Banlieues ... et ailleurs.* Paris: Armand Colin.

Chesnais, J.-C. 1981. *Histoire de la violence.* Paris: Robert Laffont.

Clément, F.; Girardin, A. 1997. *Enseigner aux élèves issus de l'immigration.* Paris: Nathan.

Collot, A.; Didier, G.; Loueslati, B. (eds.). 1993. "La pluralité culturelle dans les systèmes éducatifs européens". In: *Documents - Actes et rapports pour l'Education*, CRDP.: Lorraine.

Council for Cultural Co-operation. 1988. *Les persécutions entre enfants à l'école.* Strasbourg.

Council of Europe. 1987. *Les nouveaux défis pour les enseignants et leur formation.* Strasbourg.

Council of Europe. 1997. *Ecole et violence.* Strasbourg.

Davisse, A.; Rochex, J.-Y. 1995. *Pourvu qu'ils m'écoutent.* Créteil: Centre Régional de Documentation Pédagogique.

Debarbieux, E. 1996. *La violence en mileu scolaire (1) : Etat des lieux.* Paris:E.S.F. éditeur.

Delgado-Gaitan, C.; Trueba, H.-T. 1991. *Crossing cultural borders: education for immigrant families in America.* New York: Falmer Press.

Dumay, J.-M. 1994. *L'école agressée.* Paris: Belfond.

Dupuy-Walker, L. 1990. "Les incidents critiques et la prise de fonction des enseignants stagiaires". In: *Actes du 6ᵉ colloque de l'A.I.R.P.E.*, Sèvres. Belgium: University of Mons.

European Trade Union Committee for Education/ETUCE. 1994. *La formation des enseignants en Europe.* Brussels.

EURYDICE. 1991. *La formation initiale des Enseignants.* Brussels.

EURYDICE. 1994. *Measures to combat failure at school: a challenge for the construction of Europe.* Brussels.

Farkas, G.; Grobe, R.; Sheehan, D.; Shuan, Y. 1990. "Cultural resources and school success: gender, ethnicity and poverty group within an urban school district". In: *American Sociological Review*, Vol. 55 (1), pp. 127-142.

Fotinos, G.; Poupelin, M. 1995. *La violence à l'école : Etat de la situation en 1994 ; analyses et recommandations*. Paris: Ministère de l'Education nationale.

Gillborn, D. 1996. "Ethnicity and educational performance in the United Kingdom: racism, ethnicity and poverty group within an urban school district". In: *Anthropology and Education Quarterly*. Vol. 27(4).

Hebert, J. 1991. *La violence à l'école - Guide de prévention et techniques d'intervention*. Montréal: les éditions Logiques.

Hester, S. 1991. "The social facts of deviance in school: a study of mundane reason". In: *British Journal of Sociology*, Vol. 42, pp. 443-462.

Institut des hautes études de la sécurité intérieure (IHESI). 1994. "La violence à l'école". In: *Cahiers de la sécurité intérieure*. N° 15. Paris.

International Labour Office (ILO). 1991. *Le personnel enseignant, le défi des années 1990*. Geneva.

Leclercq, J.M. 1993. *L'enseignement secondaire obligatoire en Europe*. Paris: La Documentation Française.

Lynch, J. 1983. *The multicultural curriculum*. London:Batsford.

Malewska-Peyre, H.; Basdevant, C. *et al.* 1982. *Crise d'identité et déviance chez les jeunes immigrés*, CFRES Vaucresson. Paris: La Documentation Française.

Maniganda. 1993. "La problématique de l'enfant d'origine étrangère : nécessité de changer d'approche". In: *Revue Française de Pédagogie*. N° 104, pp.41-53.

Ministère de l'Education nationale. 1989. "Circulaire du 12 décembre 1989". In: *Bulletin officiel de l'éducation nationale*. N° 46, pp.3065-3068.

Ministère de l'Education nationale. 1992. Direction de l'Evaluation et de la Prospective, "Profession Enseignant : les débuts d'un métier". In: *Education et Formations*. N° 20. Paris.

Ministère de l'Education nationale. 1994a. Direction de l'Evaluation et de la Prospective, "Enseigner dans les collèges et les lycées". In: *Education et Formations*. N° 48, Paris.

Ministère de l'Education nationale. 1994b. "Circulaire du 20 septembre 1994 relative au port de signes ostentatoires dans les établissements scolaires". In: *Bulletin officiel de l'éducation nationale*. N° 35, pp.2528.

NAMES. 1989. "Talking it out: students mediate disputes". In: *The Harvard Education Letter.*

OECD. 1990. *L'enseignement aujourd'hui : fonctions, statuts, politiques.* Paris.

OECD. 1994. *L'école, une affaire de choix.* Paris.

Ogbu, J. 1974. *The next generation. An ethnography of education in an urban neighbourhood.* New York: Academic Press.

Ogbu, J. 1978. *Minority education and caste: The American system in a cross-cultural perspective.* New York: Academic Press.

Ogbu, J. 1987. "Variability in minority school performance: A problem in search of an explanation". In: *Anthropology and Education Quarterly.* Vol. 18 (4), pp.312-334.

Partington, G. 1985. "Multiculturalism and the common curriculum debate". In: *British Journal of Educational Studies.* Vol. 33(1), pp. 35-56.

Payet, J.-P. 1989. "L'action éducative entre école et familles". In: *Les annales de la recherche urbaine.* N° 41, pp. 97-103.

Payet, J.-P.; Van Zanten, A. 1996. "L'école, les enfants de l'immigration et des minorités ethniques". In: *Revue Française de Pédagogie.* N° 117, pp. 87-149.

Plowden Report. 1967. *Children and their primary schools*, Central Advisory Council for Education. London: HMSO.

Quivy, R.; Ruquoy, D.; Van Campenhoudt, D. 1989. *Malaise à l'école, les difficultés de l'action collective.* Brussels: Publications des facultés Universitaires Saint-Louis.

Rampton Report. 1981. Committee of Inquiry into the Education of children from ethnic minority groups. London: Department of Education and Science. *West Indian children in our schools.* London: HMSO.

Regnault, E. 1994. "Perception du soutien scolaire par des parents maghrébins migrants". In: *Formation.* N° 97, pp.155-170.

Rosenfeld, G. 1971. *"Shut those thick lips": a study of slum school failure.* Illinois: Waweland Press.

Secretary of State for Education, The Netherlands. 1994. *Newsletter.* November 1994.

Slawski, E.; Scherer, J. 1979. "The rhetoric of concern: trust and control in an urban desegregated school". In: *Anthropoly and Education Quarterly.* Vol. 9(4), pp. 258-272.

Swann Report. 1985. *Education for all. The Report of the Committee of Inquiry into the Education of children from ethnic minority groups.* London: Department of Education and Science, HMSO.

Taylor, M. 1981. *Caught between. A Review of the research into the education of pupils of West Indian origins.* Windsor: NFER-Nelson.

Thebault, J. 1995. *Le système éducatif de l'Angleterre et du pays de Galles.* Sèvres: Comité international d'Etudes Pédagogiques.

Tomlinson, S. 1983. *Ethnic minorities in British schools. A Review of the literature 1960-1982.* London: Heinemann.

Troyna, B. 1987. "Beyond multiculturalism. Towards the enactment of anti-racist education in policy, provision and pedagogy". In: *Oxford Review of Education.* Vol. 13, pp. 307-320.

Vallet, L.A. 1996. "L'assimilation scolaire des enfants issus de l'immigration et son interprétation : un examen sur données françaises". In: *Revue Française de Pédagogie*. N° 117, pp. 7-27.

Vallet, L.A.; Caille, J.-P. 1996. "Les élèves étrangers ou issus de l'immigration dans l'école et le collège français. Une étude d'ensemble". In: *Les dossiers d'Education et Formations*. N° 67. Paris.

Veenmann, S. 1984. "Perceived problems of beginning teachers". In: *Review of Educational Research*. Vol. 54, No. 2, pp. 143-178.

Walker, J. 1992. *Violence et résolution des conflits*. Strasbourg: Council of Europe.

Wentzel, K.L. 1991. "Social competences at school: relation between social responsibility and academic achievement". In: *Review of Educational Research*. Vol. 61, pp. 10-24.

Wright, C. 1987. "Black students-white teachers". In: B. Troyna (ed.). *Racial Inequality in Education*. London: Tavistock.

IIEP Publications and Documents

More than 1,200 titles on all aspects of educational planning have been published by the International Institute for Educational Planning. A comprehensive catalogue, giving details of their availability, includes research reports, case studies, seminar documents, training materials, occasional papers and reference books in the following subject categories:

Economics of education, costs and financing.

Manpower and employment.

Demographic studies.

Location of schools (school map) and micro-planning.

Administration and management.

Curriculum development and evaluation.

Educational technology.

Primary, secondary and higher education.

Vocational and technical education.

Non-formal, out-of-school, adult and rural education.

Disadvantaged groups.

Copies of the catalogue may be obtained from **IIEP Publications** on request.